INDIA's GREATEST SPEECHES

Nitin Agarwal

INDIA's GREATEST SPEECHES

Nitin Agarwal

GRAPEVINE INDIA

Grapevine India Publishers Pvt. Ltd.
Plot No.4, First Floor
Pandav Nagar
Opposite Shadipur Metro Station
Patel Nagar
New Delhi - 110008
India
grapevineindiapublishers@gmail.com
contact@grapevineindia.com

Assisted by Ashna Banga

Printed and bound in India by Thomson Press India Ltd.

To all forthcoming
torch bearers

CONTENTS

Bhagavad Gita

The Bhagavad Gita is the most revered religious book in Hinduism, widely accepted by people of different religious sentiments for its philosophical and moral relevance. It is considered to be the 'divine voice of God', for it is said that one can be spiritually uplifted by contemplating and meditating on the Gita's text. Having influenced many great thinkers over the years, the Gita is understood to be the ultimate guide with practical instructions, with its relevance understood even in these modern times.

The verses in Bhagavad Gita represent Lord Krishna's speech to Arjuna at the beginning of the battle for his kingdom. Arjuna was the best archer and a Pandava, fighting against the injustice caused by his evil relatives who had taken away his kingdom. Krishna's words had inspired him as he prepared for the battle. It originally occurred in the Bhishma Parva of the Mahabharata, comprising 18 chapters from 25 to 42. Considered the original sacred ancient knowledge, it was first transferred from Surya to King Ishvaku, before disappearing from the sands of time. It later resurfaced in this speech by Lord Krishna.

The Gita, or the 'Song of the God', is a true scripture of

the human race, with wisdom applicable across generations and races. It has inspired millions with its frankly mystical and emotional content and offers something of value to every seeker. It is considered to be a handbook for self-realization and a guide to action. Presented here is a summary of the speech, with the central messages that are universal in nature and touch everyone with their depth of meaning.

When we started off with the concept of this book, we began with acknowledging the Gita as the greatest speech ever. The lessons in context to its sheer significance in the awakening of humankind compelled us to begin from this speech. Including the entire text would have generated a huge volume, so we have collated the ten summarized teachings that are relevant in all times. Krishna, we believe, is our most revered orator, followed by the wonderful twenty who we have attempted to bring together. We hope each of you would find inspiration in these enriching words.

- Why do you worry without cause? Whom do you fear without reason? Who can kill you? The soul is neither born, nor does it die.

- Whatever happened, happened for the good; whatever is happening, is happening for the good; whatever will happen, will also happen for the good only. You need not have any regrets for the past. You need not worry for the future. The present is happening.

- What did you lose that you cry about? What did you bring with you, which you think you have lost? What did you produce, which you think got destroyed? You did not bring anything. Whatever you have, you received from here. Whatever you have given, you have given only here. Whatever you took, you took from God. Whatever you gave, you gave to him. You came empty handed, you will leave empty handed. What is yours today, belonged to someone else yesterday, and will belong to someone else the day after tomorrow. You are mistakenly enjoying the thought that this is yours. It is this false happiness that is the cause of your sorrows.

- Change is the law of the universe. What you think of as death, is indeed life. In one instance you can be a millionaire, and in the other instance you can be steeped in poverty. Yours and mine, big and small - erase these ideas from your mind. Then everything is yours and you belong to everyone.

- This body is not yours, neither are you of the body. The body is made of fire, water, air, earth and ether, and will disappear into these elements. But the soul is permanent - so who are you?

- Dedicate your being to God. He is the one to be ultimately relied upon. Those who know of his support are forever free from fear, worry and sorrow.

- Whatever you do, do it as a dedication to God. This will bring you the tremendous experience of joy and life-freedom forever.

- Whenever there will be evil, God will take over.

SWAMI VIVEKANANDA

1893

The Chicago Address
(Opening Day)

In his best-known speech at the Parliament of the World's Religions, Chicago on September 11, 1893, Swami Vivekananda formally represented Hinduism and India. It was the first session of The Parliament of World's Religions at the Art Institute of Chicago, where Vivekananda began his short speech by addressing "Sisters and Brothers of America". This was followed by a two-minute standing ovation from the seven thousand people in attendance.

In this address, he spoke of Hinduism as a religion, and of how he's a proud citizen of India, a country that has accepted refugees and sheltered them. He implied the importance of religion in a world plagued with demons in different forms. Such was the impact of this 30-year old Hindu monk's short, yet powerful speech, that he was invited by the several thousand delegates, most of who were Christian, to speak five times over the next two weeks, where he talked about Hinduism, Buddhism and harmony of religions, focusing on presenting the core value of Hinduism: universality and religious tolerance. President of the Parliament, John Henry Barrows, speaking about this address said, "India, the Mother of religions was represented by Swami Vivekananda, the orange-monk who exercised the most wonderful influence over his auditors."

What is little known is how Vivekananda reached the Parliament. He was not known during that time, and had travelled to Chicago with the help of money earned door-to-door and through donations from three South Indian kings. He realized that since he wasn't associated with any organization, and had no credentials, he couldn't register as a delegate. Having no money to go back to India and two months away from the Parliament, he met a lady on a train to Boston, who invited him to stay in her country home, moved by his story. He met people who were impressed by him and with everyone's efforts, was able to register as a delegate. Speaking confidently and addressing other delegates in English, he was an impressive sight and caused a stir in the news and media.

The Chicago Address (Opening Day), 1893

Sisters and Brothers of America,

It fills my heart with joy unspeakable to rise in response to the warm and cordial welcome which you have given us. I thank you in the name of the most ancient order of monks in the world; I thank you in the name of the mother of religions; and I thank you in the name of the millions and millions of Hindu people of all classes and sects.

My thanks, also, to some of the speakers on this platform who, referring to the delegates from the Orient, have told you that these men from far-off nations may well claim the honour of bearing to different lands the idea of toleration. I am proud to belong to a religion which has taught the world both tolerance and universal acceptance. We believe not only in universal toleration, but we accept all religions as true. I am proud to belong to a nation which has sheltered the persecuted and the refugees of all religions and all nations of the earth. I am proud to tell you that we have gathered in our bosom the purest remnant of the Israelites, who came to the southern India and took refuge with us in the very year in which their holy temple was shattered to pieces by Roman tyranny. I am proud to belong to the religion which has sheltered and is still fostering the remnant of the grand Zoroastrian nation. I will quote to you, brethren, a few lines from a hymn which I remember to have repeated from my earliest boyhood, which is every day repeated by millions of human beings:

'As the different streams having their sources in different places all mingle their water in the sea, so, O Lord, the different paths which men take through different tendencies, various though they appear, crooked or straight, all lead to Thee.'

'The present convention, which is one of the most august assemblies ever held, is in itself a vindication, a declaration to the world, of the wonderful doctrine preached in the Gita:

Whosoever comes to Me, through whatsoever form, I reach him; all men are struggling through paths which in the end lead to Me.'

Sectarianism, bigotry, and its horrible descendant, fanaticism, have long possessed this beautiful earth. They have filled the earth with violence, drenched it often and often with human blood, destroyed civilization, and sent whole nations to despair. Had it not been for these horrible demons, human society would be far more advanced than it is now. But their time is come; and I fervently hope that the bell that tolled this morning in honour of this convention may be the death-knell of all fanaticism, of all persecutions with the sword or with the pen, and of all uncharitable feelings between persons wending their way to the same goal.

MAHATMA GANDHI

1912

Banaras Hindu University Speech

Fondly remembered as the Father of the Nation, Mohandas Karamchand Gandhi was a prominent figure in India's struggle for freedom from the British rule. He led many movements across the country and preached non-violence and civil disobedience against the British. He had a vision of a free India based on religious pluralism, which was challenged when the partition took place, and religious communities spread hatred against one another. In an attempt to recover some peace, he travelled to the affected areas and performed various fasts unto death to promote religious harmony.

Mahatma Gandhi had been invited by Pandit Malaviya to speak on the occasion of the opening of the Banaras Hindu University in Uttar Pradesh. Eminent people from all over India attended the event. The then Viceroy, Lord Hardinge had come specially, for he was to lay the foundation-stone of the University. As an extra precaution, police were present in large numbers and houses along the route were heavily guarded. That day, Banaras was in a state of siege.

On February 4, 1916, Gandhi had to address the audience, most of which comprised young, impressionable minds. The stage looked royal with the presence of the Maharaja of

Darbhanga sitting in a chair. Gandhi, clad in a short, coarse dhoti, Kathiawadi cloak and turban took to the stage and disturbed by the presence of so much security and luxury, began his forthright speech with a critical remark. Addressing the young college students, Gandhi also talked about language being a reflection of the self, and expressed his wish for Hindi to be gracefully accepted by Indians, rather than trying to master a foreign tongue. He promotes the idea of self-governance as the most important contributor to overall development, citing examples from his detailed observations.

During the course of this speech, he was interrupted by Annie Besant, who felt he was encouraging anarchy and violence. Gandhi had spoken of the problem of bomb throwing and political assassination and although he condemned those actions, he also sympathized with the patriotism and bravery which had prompted them.

I wish to tender my humble apology for the long delay that took place before I was able to reach this place. And you will readily accept the apology when I tell you that I am not responsible for the delay, nor is any human agency responsible for it. The fact is that I am like an animal on show and my keepers, in their over-kindness, always manage to neglect a necessary chapter in this life, and that is pure accident. In this case, they did not provide for the series of accidents that happened to us: to me, keepers, and my carriers. Hence, this delay.

Friends, under the influence of the matchless eloquence of Mrs. Besant who has just sat down, pray, do not believe that our University has become a finished product, and that all the young men who are to come to the University, that has yet to rise and come into existence, have also come and returned from it, finished citizens of a great empire. Do not go away with any such impression, and if you, the student world to which my remarks are supposed to be addressed this evening, consider for one moment that the spiritual life, for which this country is noted and for which this country has no rival, can be transmitted through the lip, pray, believe me, you are wrong. You will never be able merely through the lip, to give the message that India, I hope, will one day deliver to the world. I myself have been fed up with speeches and lectures. I accept the lectures that have been delivered here during the last two days from this category, because they are necessary.

But I do venture to suggest to you that we have now reached almost the end of our resources in speech-making; it is not enough that our ears are feasted, that our eyes are feasted, but it is necessary that our hearts have got to be touched and that our hands and feet have got to be moved.

We have been told during the last two days how necessary it is, if we are to retain our hold upon the simplicity of the Indian character, that our hands and feet should move in unison with our hearts. But this is only by way of preface. I wanted to say it is a matter of deep humiliation and shame for us that I am compelled this evening under the shadow of this great college, in this sacred city, to address my countrymen in a language that is foreign to me. I know that if I was appointed an examiner, to examine all those who have been attending during these two days this series of lectures, most of those who might be examined upon these lectures would fail. And why? Because they have not been touched.

I was present at the sessions of the great Congress in the month of December. There was a much vaster audience, and will you believe me when I tell you that the only speeches that touched the huge audience in Bombay were the speeches that were delivered in Hindustani? In Bombay, mind you, not in Banaras where everybody speaks Hindi. But between the vernaculars of the Bombay Presidency on the one hand and Hindi on the other, no such great dividing line exists as there does between English and the sister language of India; and the Congress audience was better able to follow the speakers in Hindi. I am hoping that this University will see to it that the youths who come to it will receive their instruction through the medium of their vernaculars. Our languages are the reflection of ourselves, and if you tell me that our languages are too poor to express the best thought, then say, that the sooner we are wiped out of existence the better for us. Is there a man who dreams that English can ever become the national language of India? Why this handicap on the nation? Just consider for one moment what an equal race our lads have to run with every English lad.

I had the privilege of a close conversation with some Poona professors. They assured me that every Indian youth, because he reached his knowledge through the English language, lost at least six precious years of life. Multiply that by the numbers of students turned out by our schools and colleges, and find out for yourself, how many thousand years have been lost to the nation. The charge against us is that we have no initiative. How can we have any, if we are to devote the precious years of our life to the mastery of a foreign tongue? We fail in this attempt also. Was it possible for any speaker yesterday and today to impress his audience as was possible for Mr. Higginbotham? It was not the fault of the previous speakers that they could not engage the audience. They had more than substance enough for us in their addresses. But their addresses could not go home to us. I have heard it said that after all, it is the English educated India which is leading and which is doing all the things for the nation. It would be monstrous if it were otherwise. The only education we receive is English education. Surely we must show something for it. But suppose that we had been receiving during the past fifty years, education through our vernaculars, what should we have today? We should have today a free India, we should have our educated men, not as if they were foreigners in their own land but speaking to the heart of the nation; they would be working amongst the poorest of the poor, and whatever they would have gained during these fifty years would be a heritage for the nation. Today even our wives are not the sharers in our best thought. Look at Professor Bose and Professor Ray and their brilliant researches. Is it not a shame that their researches are not the common property of the masses?

Let us now turn to another subject.

The Congress has passed a resolution about self-government, and I have no doubt that the All-India Congress Committee and the Muslim League will do their duty and come forward with some tangible suggestions. But I, for one, must frankly confess that I am not so much interested in what they will be able to produce as I am interested in anything that the student world is going to produce or the masses are going to produce. No paper contribution will ever give us self-government. No amount of speeches will ever make us fit for self-government. It is only our conduct that will fit us for it. And how are we trying to govern ourselves?

I want to think audibly this evening. I do not want to make a speech and if you find me this evening speaking without reserve, pray, consider that you are only sharing the thoughts of a man who allows himself to think audibly, and if you think that I seem to transgress the limits that courtesy imposes upon me, pardon me for the liberty I may be taking. I visited the Vishwanath temple last evening, and as I was walking through those lanes, these were the thoughts that touched me. If a stranger dropped from above on to this great temple, and he had to consider what we as Hindus were, would he not be justified in condemning us? Is not this great temple a reflection of our own character? I speak feelingly, as a Hindu. Is it right that the lanes of our sacred temple should be as dirty as they are? The houses round about are built anyhow. The lanes are tortuous and narrow. If even our temples are not models of roominess and cleanliness, what can our self-government be? Shall our temples be abodes of holiness, cleanliness and peace as soon as the English have retired from India, either of their own pleasure or by compulsion, bag and baggage?

I entirely agree with the President of the Congress that before we think of self-government, we shall have to do the necessary plodding. In every city there are two divisions, the cantonment and the city proper. The city mostly is a stinking den. But we are a people unused to city life. But if we want city life, we cannot reproduce the easy-going hamlet life. It is not comforting to think that people walk about the streets of Indian Bombay under the perpetual fear of dwellers in the storeyed building spitting upon them. I do a great deal of railway travelling. I observe the difficulty of third-class passengers. But the railway administration is by no means to blame for all their hard lot. We do not know the elementary laws of cleanliness. We spit anywhere on the carriage floor, irrespective of the thoughts that it is often used as sleeping space. We do not trouble ourselves as to how we use it; the result is indescribable filth in the compartment. The so-called better class passengers over us, their less fortunate brethren; among them I have seen the student world also, sometimes they behave no better. They can speak English and they have worn Norfolk jackets and therefore, claim the right to force their way in and command seating accommodation.

I have turned the searchlight all over, and as you have

given me the privilege of speaking to you, I am laying my heart bare. Surely we must set these things right in our progress towards self-government. I now introduce you to another scene. His Highness the Maharaja who presided yesterday over our deliberations spoke about the poverty of India. Other speakers laid great stress upon it. But what did we witness in the great pandal in which the foundation ceremony was performed by the Viceroy? Certainly it a most gorgeous show, an exhibition of jewellery, which made a splendid feast for the eyes of the greatest jeweller who chose to come from Paris. I compare with the richly bedecked noble men the millions of the poor. And I feel like saying to these noble men, "There is no salvation for India unless you strip yourselves of this jewellery and hold it in trust for your countrymen in India." I am sure it is not the desire of the King-Emperor or Lord Hardinge that in order to show the truest loyalty to our King-Emperor, it is necessary for us to ransack our jewellery boxes and to appear bedecked from top to toe. I would undertake, at the peril of my life, to bring to you a message from King George himself that he expects nothing of the kind.

Sir, whenever I hear of a great palace rising in any great city of India, be it in British India or be it in India which is ruled by our great chiefs, I become jealous at once, and say, "Oh, it is the money that has come from the agriculturists." Over seventy-five per cent of the population are agriculturists and Mr. Higginbotham told us last night in his own felicitous language, that they are the men who grow two blades of grass in the place of one. But there cannot be much spirit of self-government about us, if we take away or allow others to take away from them almost the whole of the results of their labour. Our salvation can only come through the farmer. Neither the lawyers, nor the doctors, nor the rich landlords are going to secure it.

Now, last but not the least, it is my bounden duty to refer to what agitated our minds during these two or three days. All of us have had many anxious moments while the Viceroy was going through the streets of Banaras. There were detectives stationed in many places. We were horrified. We asked ourselves, "Why this distrust?" Is it not better that even Lord Hardinge should die than live a living death? But a representative of a mighty sovereign may not. He might find it necessary to impose these detectives on us? We may foam, we may fret, we may resent, but let us not forget that India of today in her impatience has produced an army of anarchists. I myself am an anarchist, but of another type. But there is a class of anarchists amongst us, and if I was able to reach this class, I would say to them that their anarchism has no room in India, if India is to conqueror. It is a sign of fear. If we trust and fear God, we shall have to fear no one, not the Maharajas, not the Viceroys, not the detectives, not even King George.

I honour the anarchist for his love of the country. I honour him for his bravery in being willing to die for his country; but I ask him - is killing honourable? Is the dagger of an assassin a fit precursor of an honourable death? I deny it. There is no warrant for such methods in any scriptures. If I found it necessary for the salvation of India that the English should retire, that they should be driven out, I would not hesitate to declare that they would have to go, and I hope I would be prepared to die in defence of that belief. That would, in my opinion, be an honourable death. The bomb-thrower creates secret plots, is afraid to come out into the open, and when caught pays the penalty of misdirected zeal.

I have been told, "Had we not done this, had some people not thrown bombs, we should never have gained what we have got with reference to the partition movement." (Mrs. Besant: 'Please stop it.') This was what I said in Bengal when Mr. Lyon presided at the meeting. I think what I am saying is necessary. If I am told to stop I shall obey. (Turning to the Chairman) I await your orders. If you consider that by my speaking as I am, I am not serving the country and the empire I shall certainly stop. (Cries of 'Go on.') (The Chairman: 'Please, explain your object.') I am simply. . . (another interruption) My friends, please do not resent this interruption. If Mrs. Besant this evening suggests that I should stop, she does so because she loves India so well, and she considers that I am erring in thinking audibly before you young men. But even so, I simply say this: I want to purge India of this atmosphere of suspicion on either side, if we are to reach our goal; we should have an empire which is to be based upon mutual love and mutual trust. Is it not better that we talk under the shadow of this college than that we should be talking irresponsibly in our homes? I consider that it is much better that we talk these things openly. I have done so with excellent results before now. I know that there is nothing that the students do not know. I am, therefore, turning the searchlight towards us. I hold the name of my country so dear to me that I exchange these thoughts with you, and submit to you that there is no room for anarchism in India. Let us frankly and openly say whatever we want to say our rulers, and face the consequences if what we have to say does not please them. But let us not abuse.

I was talking the other day to a member of the much-abused Civil Service. I have not very much in common with the members of that Service, but I could not help admiring the manner in which he was speaking to me. He said, "Mr. Gandhi, do you for one moment suppose that all we, Civil Servants, are a bad lot, that we want to oppress the people whom we have come to govern?" "No," I said. "Then if you get an opportunity, put in a word for the much-abused Civil Service." And I am here to put in that word. Yes, many members of the Indian Civil Service are most decidedly overbearing; they are tyrannical, at times thoughtless. Many other adjectives may be used. I grant all these things and I grant also that after having lived in India for a certain number of years some of them become somewhat degraded. But what does that signify? They were gentlemen before they came here, and if they have lost some of the moral fibre, it is a reflection upon ourselves.

Just think out for yourselves, if a man who was good yesterday has become bad after having come in contact with me, is he responsible that he has deteriorated or am I? The atmosphere of sycophancy and falsity that surrounds them on their coming to India demoralizes them, as it would many of us. It is well to take the blame sometimes. If we are to receive self-government, we shall have to take it. We shall never be granted self-government. Look at the history of the British Empire and the British nation; freedom loving as it is, it will not be a party to give freedom to a people who will not take it themselves. Learn your lesson if you wish to, from the Boer War. Those who were enemies of that empire only a few years ago have now become friends.

(At this point there was an interruption and a movement on the platform to leave. The speech, therefore, ended here abruptly.)

MAHATMA GANDHI

1922

The Great Trial of 1922

One of the most prominent leaders of India's resistance to the British Raj, Mohandas Karamchand Gandhi led many movements across the country, widely spreading his ideology of a non-violent and 'true' struggle for freedom. Gandhi assumed leadership of the Indian National Congress in 1921 and campaigned across the nation for social issues such as poverty, women's rights, caste system and religion. He also propagated swaraj, or self-rule.

He had declared a satyagraha against the British, launching the civil disobedience movement. The satyagraha had to end when a mass protest held in Chauri Chaura took a violent turn. Soon after this, Gandhi was facing persecution for the first time in India, charged for sedition by the British Government. This was due to three articles published in Young India that criticized the repressive measures adopted by the government to curb struggle for independence.

This historical trial was held on March 18, 1922 in Ahmedabad, where, addressing the courtroom of the District and Sessions Judge in the Central Hall of the Government Circuit House, he pleaded guilty. His statement in reply to the accusations thrown at him is considered a 'timeless classic', as he put forth his articulate views with grandeur. About two hundred spectators in the courtroom, moved by the integrity in his words, stood up as a mark of respect for him. He stood for spiritual laws, for he believed that following the unjust Government laws would be "contrary to our manhood if we obey law contrary to our conscience." Gandhi's landmark speech, aflame with patriotic passion, demonstrates the victory of beliefs over brute force and marked a defining moment in India's fight to freedom.

Gandhi had made the following oral statement, followed by a written statement that he read:

Before I read this statement I would like to state that I entirely endorse the learned Advocate-General's remarks in connection with my humble self. I think that he has made, because it is very true and I have no desire whatsoever to conceal from this court the fact that to preach disaffection towards the existing system of Government has become almost a passion with me, and the Advocate-General is entirely in the right when he says that my preaching of disaffection did not commence with my connection with Young India but that it commenced much earlier, and in the statement that I am about to read, it will be my painful duty to admit before this court that it commenced much earlier than the period stated by the Advocate-General. It is a painful duty with me but I have to discharge that duty knowing the responsibility that rests upon my shoulders, and I wish to endorse all the blame that the learned Advocate-General has thrown on my shoulders in connection with the Bombay occurrences, Madras occurrences and the Chauri Chuara occurrences.

Thinking over these things deeply and sleeping over them night after night, it is impossible for me to dissociate myself from the diabolical crimes of Chauri Chaura or the mad outrages of Bombay. He is quite right when he says that as a man of responsibility, a man having received a fair share of education, having had a fair share of experience of this world, I should have known the consequences of every one of my acts. I know them. I knew that I was playing with fire. I ran the risk and if I was set free I would still do the same. I have felt it this morning that I would have failed in my duty, if I did not say what I said here just now.

I wanted to avoid violence. Non-violence is the first article of my faith. It is also the last article of my creed. But I had to make my choice. I had either to submit to a system which I considered had done an irreparable harm to my country, or incur the risk of the mad fury of my people bursting forth when they understood the truth from my lips. I know that my people have sometimes gone mad. I am deeply sorry for it and I am, therefore, here to submit not to a light penalty but to the highest penalty. I do not ask for mercy. I do not plead any extenuating act. I am here, therefore, to invite and cheerfully submit to the highest penalty that can be inflicted upon me for what in law is a deliberate crime, and what appears to me to be the highest duty of a citizen. The only course open to you, the Judge, is, as I am going to say in my statement, either to resign your post, or inflict on me the severest penalty if you believe that the system and law you are assisting to administer are good for the people. I do not except that kind of conversion. But by the time I have finished with my statement you will have a glimpse of what is raging within my breast to run this maddest risk which a sane man can run.

Reading the written statement: I owe it perhaps to the Indian public and to the public in England, to placate which this prosecution is mainly taken up, that I should explain why from a staunch loyalist and co-operator, I have become an uncompromising disaffectionist and non-co-operator. To the court too I should say why I plead guilty to the charge of promoting disaffection towards the Government established by law in India.

My public life began in 1893 in South Africa in troubled weather. My first contact with British authority in that country was not of a happy character. I discovered that as a man and an Indian, I had no rights. More correctly I discovered that I had no rights as a man because I was an Indian.

But I was not baffled. I thought that this treatment of Indians was an excrescence upon a system that was intrinsically and mainly good. I gave the Government my voluntary and hearty co-operation, criticizing it freely where I felt it was faulty but never wishing its destruction.

Consequently when the existence of the Empire was threatened in 1899 by the Boer challenge, I offered my services to it, raised a volunteer ambulance corps and served at several actions that took place for the relief of Ladysmith. Similarly in 1906, at the time of the Zulu 'revolt', I raised a stretcher bearer party and served till the end of the 'rebellion'. On both the occasions I received medals and was even mentioned in dispatches. For my work in South Africa I was given by Lord Hardinge a Kaisar-i-Hind gold medal. When the war broke out in 1914 between England and Germany, I raised volunteer ambulance cars in London, consisting of the then resident Indians in London, chiefly students. Its work was acknowledged by the authorities to be valuable. Lastly, in India when a special appeal was made at the war Conference in Delhi in 1918 by Lord Chelmsford for recruits, I struggled at the cost of my health to raise a corps in Kheda, and the response was being made when the hostilities ceased and orders were received that no more recruits were wanted.

In all these efforts at service, I was actuated by the belief that it was possible by such services to gain a status of full equality in the Empire for my countrymen. The first shock came in the shape of the Rowlatt Act-a law designed to rob the people of all real freedom. I felt called upon to lead an intensive agitation against it. Then followed the Punjab horrors beginning with the massacre at Jallianwala Bagh and culminating in crawling orders, public flogging and other indescribable humiliations. I discovered too that the plighted word of the Prime Minister to the Mussalmans of India regarding the integrity of Turkey and the holy places of Islam was not likely to be fulfilled. But in spite of the forebodings and the grave warnings of friends, at the Amritsar Congress in 1919, I fought for co-operation and working of the Montagu-Chemlmsford reforms, hoping that the Prime Minister would redeem his promise to the Indian Mussalmans, that the Punjab wound would be healed, and that the reforms, inadequate and unsatisfactory though they were, marked a new era of hope in the life of India.

But all that hope was shattered. The Khilafat promise was not to be redeemed. The Punjab crime was whitewashed and most culprits went not only unpunished but remained in service, and some continued to draw pensions from the Indian revenue and in some cases were even rewarded. I saw too that not only did the reforms not mark a change of heart, but they were only a method of further raining India of her wealth and of prolonging her servitude.

I came reluctantly to the conclusion that the British connection had made India more helpless than she ever was before, politically and economically. A disarmed India has no power of resistance against any aggressor if she wanted to engage, in an armed conflict with him. So much is this the case that some of our best men consider that India must take generations, before she can achieve Dominion Status. She has become so poor that she has little power of resisting famines. Before the British advent India spun and wove in her millions of cottages, just the supplement she needed for adding to her meagre agricultural resources. This cottage industry, so vital for India's existence, has been ruined by incredibly heartless and inhuman processes as described by English witness.

Little do town dwellers how the semi-starved masses of India are slowly sinking to lifelessness. Little do they know that their miserable comfort represents the brokerage they get for their work they do for the foreign exploiter, that the profits and the brokerage are sucked from the masses. Little do realize that the Government established by law in British India is carried on for this exploitation of the masses. No sophistry, no jugglery in figures, can explain away the evidence that the skeletons in many villages present to the naked eye. I have no doubt whatsoever that both England and the town dweller of India will have to answer, if there is a God above, for this crime against humanity, which is perhaps unequalled in history. The law itself in this country has been used to serve the foreign exploiter.

My unbiased examination of the Punjab Marital Law cases has led me to believe that at least ninety-five per cent of convictions were wholly bad. My experience of political cases in India leads me to the conclusion, in nine out of every ten, the condemned men were totally innocent. Their crime consisted in the love of their country. In ninety-nine cases out of hundred, justice has been denied to Indians as against Europeans in the courts of India. This is not an exaggerated picture. It is the experience of almost every Indian who has had anything to do with such cases. In my opinion, the administration of the law is thus prostituted, consciously or unconsciously, for the benefit of the exploiter.

The greater misfortune is that the Englishmen and their Indian associates in the administration of the country do not know that they are engaged in the crime I have attempted to describe. I am satisfied that many Englishmen and Indian officials honestly follow the systems devised in the world, and that India is making steady, though, slow progress. They do not know a subtle but effective system of terrorism and an organized display of force on the one hand, and the deprivation of all powers of retaliation or self-defense on the other, as emasculated the people and induced in them the habit of simulation. This awful habit has added to the ignorance and the self-deception of the administrators. Section 124 A, under which I am happily charged, is perhaps the prince among the political sections of the Indian Penal Code designed to suppress the liberty of the citizen.

Affection cannot be manufactured or regulated by law. If one has no affection for a person or system, one should be free to give the fullest expression to his disaffection, so long as he does not contemplate, promote, or incite to violence. But the section under which mere promotion of disaffection is a crime. I have studied some of the cases tried under it; I know that some of the most loved of India's patriots have been convicted under it. I consider it a privilege, therefore, to be charged under that section. I have endeavoured to give in their briefest outline the reasons for my disaffection. I have no personal ill-will against any single administrator; much less can I have any disaffection towards the King's person. But I hold it to be a virtue to be disaffected towards a Government which in its totality has done more harm to India than any previous system. India is less manly under the British rule than she ever was before. Holding such a belief, I consider it to be a sin to have affection for the system. And it has been a precious privilege for me to be able to write what I have in the various articles tendered in evidence against me.

In fact, I believe that I have rendered a service to India and England by showing in non-co-operation the way out of the unnatural state in which both are living. In my opinion, non-co-operation with evil is as much a duty as is co-operation with good. But in the past, non-co-operation has been deliberately expressed in violence to the evil-doer. I am endeavouring to show to my countrymen that violent non-co-operation only multiples evil, and that as evil can only be sustained by violence, withdrawal of support of evil requires complete abstention from violence. Non-violence implies voluntary submission to the penalty for non-co-operation with evil. I am here, therefore, to invite and submit cheerfully to the highest penalty that can be inflicted upon me for what in law is deliberate crime, and what appears to me to be the highest duty of a citizen. The only course open to you, the Judge and the assessors, is either to resign your posts and thus dissociate yourselves from evil, if you feel that the law you are called upon to administer is an evil, and that in reality I am innocent, or to inflict on me the severest penalty, if you believe that the system and the law you are assisting to administer are good for the people of this country, and that my activity is, therefore, injurious to the common weal.

SHAHEED BHAGAT SINGH

1930

Statement Before the Lahore High Court Bench

An Indian socialist and one of the most influential revolutionaries of the Indian independence movement, Bhagat Singh is often referred to as Shaheed Bhagat Singh, the word 'Shaheed' meaning 'martyr'. He was actively involved in the revolutionary activities against the British Raj. He coined the slogan, *Inquilab Zindabaad* (Long Live Revolution!), which became a war-cry in the fight for independence. To seek revenge for the death of Lala Lajpat Rai at the hands of the police, Bhagat Singh got involved in the murder of British Police officer John Saunders. Soon after that in (), 1929, along with fellow revolutionary Batukeshwar Dutt, Bhagat Singh threw two bombs inside the Central Legislative Assembly. This was done to get an opportunity by way of getting arrested and into the limelight, and get a speaking stage to publicise the cause they were fighting for. They got what they wanted, and they went about bravely spreading their message of *Inquilab Zindabaad.* While under arrest, Bhagat Singh underwent a 116-day fast, demanding equal rights for British and Indian political prisoners.

This speech was delivered in 1930 in front of a Special Tribunal in Lahore, where Bhagat Singh and his accomplices were the accused in the Lahore Conspiracy Case. He aimed at clarifying their position, to explain once again, the motive behind their actions, and to put forth his message of injustice in front of everybody. Bhagat Singh does not defend their actions, but attempts to explain the aim and spirit behind them. He talked about the importance of considering the motive behind their actions, as had been done in the past. With this point, he implied that the punishment accorded to them was because their actions were not individualistic, but directed towards the government, a body that holds supreme power. In this speech, Bhagat Singh questions the morality of their punishment, as well as the existence of a government that resorts to unjust laws. Bringing up real life as well as metaphorical examples of unjust behaviour, he attempts to put forth his point of view, even as the court nevertheless settled to have him hanged to death. Bhagat Singh, at the age of twenty-three, was convicted and subsequently executed by the British on 23 March, 1931.

Statement Before the Lahore High Court Bench, 1930

My Lords,

We are neither lawyers nor masters of English language, nor holders of degrees. Therefore, please do not expect any oratorical speech from us. We therefore pray that instead of going into the language mistakes of our statement, Your Lordships will try to understand the real sense of it.

Leaving other points to our lawyers, I will confine myself to one point only. The point is very important in this case – what were our intentions, and to what extent are we guilty? This is a very complicated question and no one will be able to express before you that height to mental elevation which inspired us to think and act in a particular manner. We want that this should be kept in mind while assessing our intentions and our offence. According to the famous jurist Solomon, one should not be punished for his criminal offence if his aim is not against law.

We had submitted a written statement in the Sessions Court. That statement explains our aim and as such, explains our intentions also. But the learned judge dismissed it with one stroke of pen, saying, "Generally, the operation of law is not affected by how or why one committed the offence. In this country, the aim of the offence is very rarely mentioned in legal commentaries." My Lords, our contention is that under the circumstances, the learned judge ought to have judged us either by the result of our action or on the basis of the psychological part of our statement. But he did not take any of these factors into consideration.

The point to be considered is that the two bombs we threw in the Assembly did not harm anybody physically or economically. As such the punishment awarded to us is not only very harsh but revengeful also. Moreover, the motive of the offence of the accused cannot be found without knowing his psychology. And no one can do justice to anybody without taking his motive into consideration. If we ignore the motive, the biggest general of the words will appear like ordinary murderers; revenue officers will look like thieves and cheats. Even judges will be accused of murder. This way the entire social system and the civilisation will be reduced to murders, thefts and cheating. If we ignore the motive, the government will have no right to expect sacrifice from its people and its officials. Ignore the motive and every religious preacher will be dubbed as a preacher of falsehoods, and every prophet will be charged of misguiding crores of simple and ignorant people.

If we set aside the motive, then Jesus Christ will appear to be a man responsible for creating disturbances, breaking peace and preaching revolt, and will be considered to be a 'dangerous personality' in the language of the law. But we worship him. He commands great respect in our hearts and his image creates vibrations of spiritualism amongst us. Why? Because the inspiration behind his actions was that of a high ideal. The rulers of that age could not recognise that high idealism. They only saw his outward actions. Nineteen centuries have passed since then. Have we not progressed during this period? Shall we repeat that mistake again? It that be so, then we shall have to admit that all the sacrifices of mankind and all the efforts of the great martyrs were useless and it would appear as if we are still at the same place where we stood twenty centuries back.

From the legal point of view also, the question of motive is of special importance. Take the example of General Dyer. He resorted to firing and killed hundreds of innocent and unarmed people. But the military court did not order him to be shot. It gave him lakhs of rupees as award. Take another example. Shri Kharag Bahadur Singh, a young Gurkha, killed a Marwari in Calcutta. If the motive be set aside, then Kharag Bahadur Singh ought to have been hanged. But he was awarded a mild sentence of a few years only. He was even released much before the expiry of his sentence. Was there any loophole in the law that he escaped capital punishment? Or, was the charge of murder not proved against him? Like us, he also accepted the full responsibility of his action, but he escaped death. He is free today. I ask Your Lordship, why was he not awarded capital punishment? His action was well calculated and well planned. From the motive end, his action was more serious and fatal than ours. He was awarded a mild punishment because his intentions were good. He saved the society from a dirty leech who had sucked the life-blood of so many pretty young girls. Kharag Singh was given a mild punishment just to uphold the formalities of the law.

This principle (that the law does not take motive into consideration) is quite absurd. This is against the basic principles of the law which declares, "The law is for man and not man for the law". As such, why are the same norms are not being applied to us as well? It is quite clear that while convicting Kharag Singh, his motive was kept in mind, otherwise a murderer can never escape the hangman's noose. Are we being deprived of the ordinary advantage of the law because our offence is against the government, or because our action has a political importance?

My Lords, under these circumstances, please permit us

to assert that a government which seeks shelter behind such mean methods has no right to exist. If it is exists, it is for the time being only, and that too with the blood of thousands of people on its head. If the law does not see the motive, there can be no justice, nor can there be stable peace.

Mixing of arsenic (poison) in flour will not be considered a crime, provided its purpose is to kill rats. But if the purpose is to kill a man, it becomes a crime of murder. Therefore, such laws which do not stand the test of reason, and which are against the principle of justice, should be abolished. Because of such unjust laws, many great intellectuals had to adopt the path of revolt.

The facts regarding our case are very simple. We threw two bombs in the legislative Assembly on April 8, 1929. As a result of the explosion, a few persons received minor scratches. There was pandemonium in the chamber; hundreds of visitors and members of the Assembly ran out. Only my friend B.K. Dutt and I remained seated in the visitors' gallery and offered ourselves for arrest. We were tried for attempt to murder, and convicted for life. As mentioned above, as a result of the bomb explosion, only four or five persons were slightly injured and one bench got damaged. We offered ourselves for arrest without any resistance. The Sessions Judge admitted that we could have very easily escaped, had that been our intention. Instead, we accepted our offence and gave a statement explaining our position. We are not afraid of punishment. But we do not want that we should be wrongly understood. The judge removed a few paragraphs from our statement. We consider this to be harmful for our real position.

A proper study of the full text of our statement will make it clear that, according to us, our country is passing through a delicate phase. We saw the coming catastrophe and thought it proper to give a timely warning with a loud voice, and we gave the warning in the manner we thought proper. We may be wrong. Our line of thinking and that of the learned judge may be different, but that does not mean that we should be deprived of the permission to express our ideas, and wrong things be propagated in our name.

In our statement we explained in detail what we mean by "Long Live Revolution" and "Down With Imperialism". That formed the crux of our ideas. That portion was removed from our statement. Generally a wrong meaning is attributed to the word 'revolution'. That is not our understanding. Bombs and pistols do not make revolution. The sword of revolution is sharpened on the whetting-stone of ideas. This is what we wanted to emphasise. By revolution, we mean the end of the miseries of capitalist wars. It was not proper to pronounce judgement without understanding our aims and objects and the process of achieving them. To associate wrong ideas with our names is out and out injustice.

It was very necessary to give the timely warning that unrest of the people is increasing and that the malady may take a serious turn if not treated in time, and properly. If our warning is not heeded, no human power will be able to stop it. We took this step to give proper direction to the storm. We are serious students of history. We believe that, had the ruling powers acted correctly at the proper time, there would have been no bloody revolutions in France and Russia. Several big powers of the world tried to check the storm of ideas and were sunk in the atmosphere of bloodshed. Ruling people cannot change the flow of the current. We wanted to give the first warning. Had we aimed at killing some important personalities, we would have failed in the attainment of our aim.

My Lords, this was the aim and the spirit behind our action, and the result of the action corroborates our statement. There is one more point which needs elucidation, and that is regarding the strength of the bombs. Had we had no idea of the strength of the bombs, there would have been no question of our throwing them in the presence of our respected national leaders like Pandit Motilal Nehru, Shri Kelkar, Shri Jayaker and Shri Jinnah. How could we have risked the lives of our leaders? After all, we are not mad and had we been so, we would have certainly been sent to the lunatic asylum, instead of being put in jail. We had full knowledge about the strength of the bombs and that is why we acted with so much confidence. It was very easy to have thrown the bombs on the occupied benches, but it was difficult to have thrown them on unoccupied seats. Were we not of saner minds or had we been mentally unbalanced, the bombs would have fallen on occupied benches and not in empty places. Therefore, I would say that we should be rewarded for the courage we showed in carefully selecting the empty places. Under these conditions, My Lords, we think we have not been understood properly. We have not come before you to get our sentences reduced. We have come here to clarify our position. We want that we should not be given any unjust treatment, nor should any unjust opinion be pronounced about us. The question of punishment is of secondary importance before us.

V.D. SAVARKAR

1937

Presidential Address, Akhil Bharatiya Hindu Mahasabha

Vinayak Damodar Savarkar is a prominent name in Indian politics as the one who advocated dismantling the system of caste in Hindu culture. He was an Indian activist, politician, poet, writer and playwright. He created the term Hindutva, and emphasised its distinctiveness from Hinduism which he associated with social and political communalism. The aim of Hindutva was to create an inclusive collective identity. The five elements of his philosophy were: Utilitarianism, Rationalism and Positivism, Humanism and Universalism, Pragmatism and Realism. However, although his philosophy claimed to promote unity, some critics have stated that it was divisive in nature, and tried shaping Indian nationalism majorly on the basis of Hinduism.

V.D. Savarkar gave the Presidential Address at the 19th Session of the Hindu Mahasabha at Karnavati (Ahmedabad), 1937. In this abridged version of the speech, V.D. Savarkar talks broadly about the sacred cause of Hindustan, and dealt with some fundamental aspects of the Hindu Sanghatan Movement. He defined the term 'Hindutva' in an attempt to clear any misunderstanding of the term as associated with a particular religion, defining it as belonging to a wider meaning, and diverse group of people. He spoke about what Hinduism stands for, with respect to the country as a whole and what it represents.

Talking at length about the movement by the Hindu Mahasabha, he explained how it is not a religious, but a national body. He defended the movement and the just and fundamental rights of the people of the nation against overbearing aggression.

Presidential Address, Akhil Bharatiya Hindu Mahasabha

Ladies and Gentlemen,

I thank you most cordially for the trust you have placed in me in calling upon me to preside on this 19th Session of the Hindu Mahasabha. I don't take it so much as an honour bestowed upon me by my nation for service rendered in the past as a command to dedicate whatever strength is still left in me to the Sacred Cause of defending Hindudom and Hindustan, our common Motherland and our common Holyland, and pressing on the fight for our National Freedom. So far as the Hindus are concerned there can be no distinction or conflict in the least between our Communal and National duties, as the best interests of Hindudom are simply identified with best interests of Hindustan as a whole. Hindudom cannot advance or fulfil its life mission unless and until our Motherland is set free and consolidated into an Indian State in which all our countrymen, to whatever religion or sect or race they belong, are treated with perfect equality and none allowed to dominate others or is deprived of his just and equal rights of free citizenship, as long as everyone discharges the common obligations and duties which one owes to the Indian Nation as a whole. The truer a Hindu is to himself, as a Hindu he must inevitably grow a truer National as well. I shall substantiate this point later on as I proceed.

With this conviction and from this point of view, I shall deal in my presidential address with some fundamental aspects of the Hindu Sanghatan Movement as expounded by this Mahasabha or as I understand them and leave detailed and passing questions, to be deliberated upon and decided, to the representatives assembled in this Session.

Homage to the Independent Hindu, Kingdom of Nepal

But before proceeding further I feel it my bounden duty to send forth on behalf of all Hindus our loyal and loving greetings to His Majesty the King of Nepal, His Highness Shree Yuddhsamasher Ranajee - the Prime Minister of Nepal and all of our co-religionists and countrymen there who have even in the darkest hour of our history, been successful in holding out as Hindu Power and in keeping a flag of Hindu Independence flying unsullied on the summits of the Himalayas. The Kingdom of Nepal stands out today as the only Hindu Kingdom in the world whose independence is recognised by England, France, Italy and other great powers. Amongst some twenty-five crores of our Hindus in this generation, His Majesty the King of Nepal is the first and foremost and the only Hindu today who can enter in the assemblage of King, Emperors and Presidents of all the independent nations in the world, with head erect and unbent, as an equal amongst equals. In spite of the passing political aspect of the question, Nepal is bound to Hindudom as a whole by the dearest ties of a common race and religion and language and culture, inheriting with us our common Motherland and our common Holyland. Our life is one. Whatever contributes to the strength of Hindudom as a whole, must strengthen Nepal and whatever progress the latter records is bound to elevate the first. Hence all Sanghatanist Hindus long to see that the only Independent Hindu Kingdom is rapidly brought to an up-to-date efficiency, political social, and above all military and aerial so as to enable Her to hold out Her own in the National struggle for existence that is going on all around us and march on and fulfil the great and glorious destiny that awaits Her ahead.

Message of Sympathy to the Hindus in the Greater Hindustan

Nor can this session of the Hindu Mahasabha forget to send forth its message of sympathy and loving remembrances to those of our co-religionists and countrymen abroad, who have been building a greater Hindustan without the noise of drums and trumpets in Africa, America, Mauritius and such other parts of the world, and also to those who, in the island of Bali, are still holding out as remnants of the ancient world Empire of our Hindu Race.

Their fortune too is inextricably bound up with the freedom and strength and greatness of Bharatavarsha which is the 'Pitrubhoo' and 'Punyabhoo' - the Fatherland and the Holyland of Hindudom as a whole. Hindustan must ever remain one and indivisible.

Nor can the Hindu Mahasabha afford to be forgetful of the Hindus who reside in the so-called 'French India' and 'Portuguese India' in India! The very words sound preposterous and insulting to us. Apart from the artificial and enforced political divisions of today, we are indissolubly bound together by the enduring ties of blood and religion and country. We must declare, as an ideal at any rate, that Hindustan of tomorrow must be one and indivisible not only a united but a unitarian nation, from Kashmir to Rameshwar, from Sindh to Assam. I hope that not only the Mahasabha but even the Congress and such other national bodies in Hindustan will not fight shy of claiming Gomantak, Pondicherry, and such other parts of Hindustan as parts as inalienable and integral of our Nation as is Maharashtra or Bengal or Punjab.

The definition of the word 'Hindu'

As a whole superstructure of the mission and the function of the Hindu Mahasabha rests on the correct definition of the word 'Hindu,' we must first of all make it clear what 'Hindutva' really means. Once the scope and the meaning of the world is defined and understood, a number of misgivings in our own camp are easily removed, a number of misunderstandings and objections raised against us from the camp of our opponents are met and silenced. Fortunately for us, after a lot of wandering in wilderness, a definition of the word Hindu which is not only historically and logically as sound as is possible in the cases of such comprehensive terms, but is also eminently workable is already hit upon when 'Hindutva' was defined as :-

।। आसिंधूसिंधूपयता [यःय भारतभूमिका ।।
।। ŏपतृभूःपुÖयभूयैठैव स वैŏहंदारतिःम¸ तः¸ ।।

'Everyone who regards and claims this Bharatbhoomi from the Indus to the Seas as his Fatherland and Holyland is a Hindu.'

Here I must point out that it is rather loose to say that any person professing any religion of Indian origin is a Hindu. Because that is only one aspect of Hindutva. The second and equally essential constituent of the concept of Hindutva cannot be ignored if we want to save the definition from getting overlapping and unreal. It is not enough that a person should profess any religion of Indian origin, i.e., Hindustan as his Holyland, but he must also recognise it as his Fatherland as well.

As this is no place for going into the whole discussion of the pros and cons of the question, all I can do here is to refer to my book 'Hindutva' in which I have set forth all arguments and expounded the proposition at great length. I shall content myself at present by stating that Hindudom is bound and marked out as a people and a nation by themselves not by the only tie of a common Holyland in which their religion took birth but by the ties of a common culture, a common language, a common history and essentially of a common fatherland as well. It is these two constituents taken together that constitute our Hindutva and distinguish us form any other people in the world.

That is why the Japanese and the Chinese, for example, do not and cannot regard themselves as fully identified with the Hindus. Both of them regard our Hindustan as their Holyland, the land which was the cradle of their religion, but they do not and cannot look upon Hindustan as their fatherland too. They are our co-religionists; but are not and cannot be our countrymen too. We Hindus are not only co-religionists, but even countrymen of each other. The Japanese and the Chinese have a different ancestry, language, culture, history and country of their own, which are not so integrally bound up with us as to constitute a common national life. In a religious assembly of the Hindus, in any Hindu Dharma-Mahasabha they can join with us as our brothers-in-faith having a common Holyland. But they will not and cannot take a common part or have a common interest in a Hindu Mahasabha which unites Hindus together and represent their national life. A definition must in the main respond to reality. Just as by the first constituent of Hindutva, the possession of a common Holyland - the Indian Mahommedans, Jews, Christians, Parsees, etc. are excluded from claiming themselves as Hindus which in reality also they do not – in spite of their recognising Hindustan as their fatherland, so also on the other hand the second constituent of the definition, that of possessing a common fatherland exclude the Japanese, the Chinese and others from the Hindu fold in spite of the fact of their having a Holyland in common with us. The above definition had already been adopted by number of prominent Hindu-sabhas such as the Nagpur, Poona, Ratnagiri Hindu-sabhas, and others.

The Hindu Mahasabha also had in view this very definition when the word Hindu was rather loosely explained in its present constitution as ' one who profess any religion of Indian origin.' I submit that the time has come when we should be more accurate and replace that partial description by regular definition and incorporate in the constitution the full verse itself translating it in the precise terms as rendered above.

Avoid the loose and harmful misuse of the word 'Hindu'

From this correct definition of Hindutva it necessarily follows that we should take all possible care to restrict the use of the word 'Hindu' to its defined and definite general meaning only and avoid misusing it in any sectarian sense. In common parlance even our esteemed leaders and writers who on the one hand are very particular in emphasizing that our non-Vedic religious schools are also included in the common Hindu brotherhood, commit on the other hand, the serious mistake of using such expressions as 'Hindus and Sikhs', 'Hindus and Jains' denoting thereby unconsciously that the Vaidiks or the Sanatanists only are Hindus and thus quite unawares inculcate the deadly virus of separation in the minds of the different constituents of our religious brotherhood, defeating our own eager desire to consolidate them all into a harmonious and organic whole. Confusion in words leads to confusion in thoughts. If we take good care not to identify the term ' Hindu ' with the major Vedic section of our people alone, our non-Vedic brethren such as the Sikhs, the Jains and others will find no just reason to resent the application of the word ' Hindu ' in their case also. Those who hold to the opinion that Sikhis, Jainism and such other religion that go to form our Hindu brotherhood are neither the branches of nor originated from the Vedas but are independent religions by themselves need not cherish any fear or suspicion of losing their independence as a religious school by being called Hindus, if that application is rightly used only to denote all those who won India, this Bharatbhoomi, as their Holyland and fatherland.

Whenever we want to discriminate the constituents of Hindudom as a whole we should designate them as 'Vaidiks and Sikhs', 'Vaidiks and Jains' etc. But to say 'Hindus and Sikhs', 'Hindus and Jains' is as self-contradictory and misleading as to say 'Hindus and Brahmins' or 'Jains and Digambers' or 'Sikhs and Akalees.' Such a harmful misuse of the word Hindu should be carefully avoided, especially in the speeches, resolutions and records of our Hindu Mahasabha.

The word 'Hindu' is of Vaidic origin

We may mention here in passing that the word 'Hindu' is not a denomination which the foreigners applied to us in contempt otherwise but is derived from our Vedic appellation of Saptasindhus, a fact which is fully dealt with in my book on Hindutva and is borne out by the name of one of our provinces and peoples bordering on the Indus who are being called down to this day as Sindh and Sindhi.

The Hindu Mahasabha is in the main not a religious but a national body. From this above discussion it necessarily follows that the concept of the term 'Hindutva'-Hinduness-is more comprehensive than the word 'Hinduism'. It was to draw a pointed attention to this distinction that I had coined the words 'Hindutva', 'Pan Hindu' and 'Hindudom' when I framed the definition of the word 'Hindu'. Hinduism concerns with the religious systems of the Hinds, their theology and dogma. But this is precisely a matter which this Hindu Mahasabha leaves entirely to individual or group conscience and faith. The Mahasabha takes its stand on no dogma, no book or school of philosophy whether pantheist, monotheist or atheist. All that it is concerned with, so far as 'ism' is concerned, is the common characteristic, which a Hindu, by the very fact of professing allegiance to a religion or faith of Indian origin necessarily possesses in regarding India as his Holyland.

This, while only indirectly concerned with Hinduism, is only one of the many aspects of Hindutva resulting from the second constituent of possessing a common Fatherland. The Mahasabha is not in the main a Hindu-Dharma-Sabha but it is pre-eminently a HinduRashtra-Sabha and is a Pan-Hindu organization shaping the destiny of the Hindu Nation in all its social, political and cultural aspects. Those who commit the serious mistake of taking the Hindu Mahasabha for only a religious body would do well to keep those distinctions in mind.

The Hindus are a Nation by themselves

Some cavil at the position I have taken that the Hindu Mahasabha as I understand its mission, is pre-eminently a national body and challenge me-'How the Hindus who differ so much amongst themselves in every detail of life could at all be called a nation as such?' To them my reply is that no people on the earth are as homogenous as to present perfect uniformity in language, culture, race and religion. A people is marked out a nation by themselves not so much by the absence of any heterogeneous differences amongst themselves as by the fact of their differing from other peoples more markedly than they differ amongst themselves. Even those who deny the fact that the Hindus could be called a nation by themselves, do recognise Great Britain, the United States, Russia, Germany and other peoples as nations. What is the test by which those peoples are called nations by themselves? Take Great Britain as an example. There are at any rate three different languages there; they have fought amongst themselves dreadfully in the past, there are to be found the traces of different seeds and bloods and race. If you say that in spite of it all they are a nation because they possess a common country, a common language, a common culture and common Holyland, then the Hindus too possess a common country so well marked out as Hindustan, a common language - Sanskrit - from which all their current languages are derived or are nourished and which forms even today the common language of their scriptures and literature and which is held in esteem as the sacred reservoir of ancient scriptures and the tongue of their forefathers.

By 'Anuloma' and 'Pratiloma' marriages their seed and blood continued to get commingled even since the days of Manu. Their social festivals and cultural forms are not less common than those we find in England. They possess a common Holyland. The Vedic Rishis are their common pride, their Grammarians Panini and Patanjali, their Poets Bhavabhooti and Kalidas, their heroes Shri Ram and Shri Krishna, Shivaji and Pratap, Guru Govind and Banda are a source of common inspiration. Their Prophets Buddha and Mahaveer, Kanad and Shankar, are held in common esteem. Like their ancient and sacred language-the Sanskrit-their scripts also are fashioned on the same basis and the Nagari script has been the common vehicle of their sacred writings since centuries in the past. Their ancient and modern history is common. They have friends and enemies in common. They have faced common dangers and won victories in common. One in national glory and one in national disasters, one in national despairs and one in national hope and Hindus are welded together during aeons of a common life and a common habitat. Above all the Hindus are bound together by the dearest, most sacred and most enduring bonds of a common Fatherland and a common Holyland, and these two being identified with one and the same country our Bharatbhumi, our India, the National Oneness and homogenity of the Hindus have been doubly sure.

If the United States with the warring crowds of Negroes, Germans and Anglo-saxons, with a common past not exceeding four or five centuries put together can be called a nation-then the Hindus must be entitled to be recognized as a nation par excellence. Verily the Hindus as a people differ most markedly from any other people in the world than they differ amongst themselves. All tests whatsoever of a common country, race, religion, and language that go to entitle a people to form a nation, entitle the Hindus with greater emphasis to that claim. And whatever differences divide the Hindus amongst themselves are rapidly disappearing owing to their awakening of the national consciousness and the Sanghatan and the social reform movements of today.

Therefore the Hindu Mahasabha that has, as formulated in its current constitution, set before itself the task of 'the maintenance, protection and promotion of the Hindu race, culture and civilization for the advancement and glory of Hindu Rashtra' is pre-eminently a national body represent the Hindu Nation as a whole.

Is this mission of the Mahasabha narrow, anti-Indian and parochial aim?

Some of our well meaning but unthinking section of Indian patriots who look down upon the Mahasabha as a communal, narrow and anti-Indian body only because it represents Hindudom and tries to protect its just rights, forget the fact that communal and parochial are only relative terms and do not by themselves imply a condemnation or curse. Are not they themselves who swear by the name of Indian Nationalism in season and out of season liable to the same charge of parochialness? If the Mahasabha represents the Hindu nation only, they claim to represent the Indian nation alone. But is not the concept of an Indian Nation itself a parochial conception in relation to Human State? In fact the Earth is our motherland and Humanity our Nation. Nay, the Vedantist goes further and claims this Universe for his country and all manifestation from the stars to the stone his own self.

'आमचा :वदेश । भुवनऽयामÚये वास ।।' says Tukaram! Why then take the Himalayas to cut us off from the rest of mankind, deem ourselves as separate Nation as Indians and fight with every other country and the English in particular who after all are our brothers - in Humanity! Why not sacrifice Indian interests to those of the British Empire which is a larger political synthesis? The fact is that all Patriotism is more or less parochial and communal and is responsible for dreadful wars throughout human history. Thus the Indian Patriots who instead of starting and joining some movement of a universal state, stop short of it, join an Indian Movement and yet continue to mock at the Hindu Sanghatan as narrow and communal and parochial succeed only in mocking at themselves.

But if it is said justification of Indian Patriotism that the people who populate India are more akin to each other bound by ties of a common ancestry, language, culture, history, etc. than they are to any other people outside India and therefore we Indians feel it our first duty to protect our Nation from our political domination and aggression of other non-Indian nations then, the same reason could be adduced to justify the Hindu Sanghatan Movement as well.

When are national, communal, or parochial movements harmful to Humanity?

No movement is condemnable simply because it is sectional. So long as it tries to defend the just and fundamental rights of a particular nation or people or community against the unjust and overbearing aggression of other human aggregates and does not infringe on an equal just right and liberties of others, it cannot be condemned or looked down simply because the nation or community is a smaller aggregate in itself. But when a nation or community treads upon the rights of sister nations or communities and aggressively stands in the way of forming larger associations and aggregates of mankind, its nationalism or communalism becomes condemnable from a human point of view. This is the acid test of distinguishing a justifiable nationalism or communalism from an unjust and harmful one. The Hindu Sanghatan movement, call it national, communal or parochial as you like stands as much justified by this real test as our Indian Patriotism can be.

What does the Independence of India mean?

In common parlance, it is understood as the political freedom of our country, of our land, the independence of the geographical unit called India. But the time has come when these expressions must be fully analysed and understood. A country or a geographical unit does not in itself constitute a nation. Our country is endeared to us because it has been the abode of our race, our people, our dearest and nearest relations and as such is only metaphorically referred to, to express our national being. The independence of India means, therefore, the independence of our people, our race, our nation. Therefore Indian swarajya or Indian swatantrya means, as far as the Hindu Nation is concerned, the political independence of the Hindus, the freedom which would enable them to grow to their full height.

India is dear to us because it has been and is the home of our Hindu Race, the land which has been the cradle of our prophets and heroes and gods and godmen. Otherwise land for land there may be many a country as rich in gold and silver on the face of the earth. River for river the Mississippi is nearly as good as the Ganges and its waters are not altogether bitter. The stones and trees and greens in Hindustan are just as good or bad stones and trees and greens of the respective species elsewhere. Hindustan is a Fatherland and Holyland to us not because it is a land entirely unlike any other land in the world but because it is associated with our history, has been the home of our forefathers, wherein our mothers gave us the first suckle at their breast and our fathers cradled us on their knees from generation to generation.

RABINDRANATH TAGORE

1941

Civilization's Crisis, The Last Testament of Tagore

Rabindranath Tagore was a distinguished and widely respected Bengali scholar and learner, who became the first non-European to win the Nobel Prize for Literature in 1913. He is known to have reshaped Bengali literature and music, his own works being acclaimed for their lyricism, colloquialism and unique contemplation. His most popular works include Gitanjali, Gora and Ghare-Baire.

India's national anthem, Jana Gana Mana and Bangladesh's Amar Shona Bangla were composed by him. A believer in the Upanishads ideals of education, he led the Brahmo Samaj, a new religious sect in the late nineteenth century. Tagore was knighted by King George V of the ruling British Government in India, which he later renounced in response to the Jallianwala Bagh massacre in 1919.

Known to be Tagore's last testament, this speech was pronounced in Shantiniketan on April 14, 1941. It was the height of the Second World War, and in April during the Bengali New year, Tagore wrote and delivered this speech titled, 'Civilization's Crisis'. In this powerful and reflective speech, Tagore expresses his dismay over the state of affairs around him at that time. Referring to the term 'civilization' as defined in English, as well as in the traditional text by Manu, he spoke of how it had come to India and the realization that India is far from living those ideals, shook him up. He accepts how he was enchanted with English literature and later realized that civilization isn't as profound a concept, when he came to terms with Indian poverty and such realities. Even as he was nearing the end of his life, saddened by destruction among humans, he had been clinging to hope, and refusing to lose faith in man.

Civilization's Crisis, The Last Testament of Tagore, 1941

Today I complete eighty years of my life. As I look back on the vast stretch of years that lie behind me and see in clear perspective the history of my early development, I am struck by the change that has taken place both in my own attitude and in the psychology of my countrymen - a change that carries within it a cause of profound tragedy.

Our direct contact with the larger world of men was linked up with the contemporary history of the English people whom we came to know in those earlier days. It was mainly through their mighty literature that we formed our ideas with regard to these newcomers to our Indian shores. In those days the type of learning that was served out to us was neither plentiful nor diverse, nor was the spirit of scientific enquiry very much in evidence. Thus their scope being strictly limited, the educated of those days had recourse to English language and literature. Their days and nights were eloquent with the stately declamations of Burke, with Macaulay's long-rolling sentences; discussions centred upon Shakespeare's drama and Byron's poetry and above all upon the large-hearted liberalism of the nineteenth-century English politics.

At the time though tentative attempts were being made to gain our national independence, at heart we had not lost faith in the generosity of the English race. This belief was so firmly rooted in the sentiments of our leaders as to lead them to hope that the victor would of his own grace pave the path of freedom for the vanquished. This belief was based upon the fact that England at the time provided a shelter to all those who had to flee from persecution in their own country. Political martyrs who had suffered for the honour of their people were accorded unreserved welcome at the hands of the English. I was impressed by this evidence of liberal humanity in the character of the English and thus I was led to set them on the pedestal of my highest respect. This generosity in their national character had not yet been vitiated by imperialist pride. About this time, as a boy in England, I had the opportunity of listening to the speeches of John Bright, both in and outside Parliament. The large-hearted, radical liberalism of those speeches, overflowing all narrow national bounds, had made so deep an impression on my mind that something of it lingers even today, even in these days of graceless disillusionment.

Certainly that spirit of abject dependence upon the charity of our rulers was no matter for pride. What was remarkable, however, was the wholehearted way in which we gave our recognition to human greatness even when it revealed itself in the foreigner. The best and noblest gifts of humanity cannot be the monopoly of a particular race or country; its scope may not be limited nor may it be regarded as the miser's hoard buried underground. That is why English literature which nourished our minds in the past, does even now convey its deep resonance to the recesses of our heart.

It is difficult to find a suitable Bengali equivalent for the English word 'civilization'. That phase of civilization with which we were familiar in this country has been called by Manu 'Sadachar' (literally, proper conduct), that is, the conduct prescribed by the tradition of the race. Narrow in themselves these time-honoured social conventions originated and held good in a circumscribed geographical area, in that strip of land, Brahmavarta by name, bound on either side by the rivers Saraswati and Drisadvati. That is how a pharisaic formalism gradually got the upper hand of free thought and the ideal of 'proper conduct' which Manu found established in Brahmavarta steadily degenerated into socialized tyranny.

During my boyhood days the attitude towards the cultured and educated section of Bengal, nurtured on English learning, was charged with a feeling of revolt against these rigid regulations of society. A perusal of what Rajnarain Bose has written describing the ways of the educated gentry of those days will amply bear out what I have said just now. In place of these set codes of conduct we accepted the ideal of 'civilization' as represented by the English term.

In our own family this change of spirit was welcomed for the sake of its sheer rational and moral force and its influence was felt in every sphere of our life. Born in that atmosphere, which was moreover coloured by our intuitive bias for literature, I naturally set the English on the throne of my heart. Thus passed the first chapters of my life. Then came the parting of ways accompanied with a painful feeling of disillusion when I began increasingly to discover how easily those who accepted the highest truths of civilization disowned them with impunity whenever questions of national self-interest were involved.

There came a time when perforce I had to snatch myself away from the mere appreciation of literature. As I emerged into the stark light of bare facts, the sight of the dire poverty of the Indian masses rent my heart. Rudely shaken out of my dreams, I began to realize that perhaps in no other modern state was there such hopeless dearth of the most elementary needs of existence. And yet it was this country whose resources had fed for so long the wealth and magnificence of the British people. While I was lost in the contemplation of the great world of civilization, I could never have remotely imagined that the great ideals of humanity would end in such ruthless travesty. But today a glaring example of it stares me in the face in the utter and contemptuous indifference of a so-called civilized race to the wellbeing of crores of Indian people.

That mastery over the machine, by which the British have consolidated their sovereignty over their vast Empire, has been kept a sealed book, to which due access has been denied to this helpless country. And all the time before our very eyes Japan has been transforming herself into a mighty and prosperous nation. I have seen with my own eyes the admirable use to which Japan has put in her own country the fruits of this progress. I have also been privileged to witness, while in Moscow, the unsparing energy with which Russia has tried to fight disease and illiteracy, and has succeeded in steadily liquidating ignorance and poverty, wiping off the humiliation from the face of a vast continent. Her civilization is free from all invidious distinction between one class and another, between one sect and another. The rapid and astounding progress achieved by her made me happy and jealous at the same time.

One aspect of the Soviet administration which particularly pleased me was that it provided no scope for unseemly conflict of religious differences, nor set one community against another by unbalanced distribution of political favours. That

I consider a truly civilized administration which impartially serves the common interests of the people.

While other imperialist powers sacrifice the welfare of the subject races to their own national greed, in the USSR I found a genuine attempt being made to harmonise the interests of the various nationalities that are scattered over its vast area. I saw peoples and tribes, who, only the other day, were nomadic savages being encouraged and indeed trained, to avail themselves freely of the benefits of civilization. Enormous sums are being spent on their education to expedite the process. When I see elsewhere some two hundred nationalities - which only a few years ago were at vastly different stages of development - marching ahead in peaceful progress and amity, and when I look about my own country and see a very highly evolved and intellectual people drifting into the disorder of barbarism, I cannot help contrasting the two systems of governments, one based on co-operation, the other on exploitation, which have made such contrary conditions possible.

I have also seen Iran, newly awakened to a sense of national self sufficiency, attempting to fulfil her own destiny freed from the deadly grinding-stones of two European powers. During my recent visit to that country I discovered to my delight that Zoroastrians who once suffered from the fanatical hatred of the major community and whose rights had been curtailed by the ruling power were now free from this age-long repression, and that civilized life had established itself in the happy land. It is significant that Iran's good fortune dates from the day when she finally disentangled herself from the meshes of European diplomacy. With all my heart I wish Iran well.

Turning to the neighbouring kingdom of Afghanistan I find that though there is much room for improvement in the field of education and social development, yet she is fortunate in that she can look forward to unending progress; for none of the European powers, boastful of their civilization, has yet succeeded in overwhelming and crushing her possibilities.

Thus while these other countries were marching ahead, India, smothered under the dead weight of British administration, lay static in her utter helplessness. Another great and ancient civilization for whose recent tragic history the British cannot disclaim responsibility, is China. To serve their own national profit the British first doped her people with opium and then appropriated a portion of her territory. As the world was about to forget the memory of this outrage, we were painfully surprised by another event. While Japan was quietly devouring North China, her act of wanton aggression was ignored as a minor incident by the veterans of British diplomacy. We have also witnessed from this distance how actively the British statesmen acquiesced in the destruction of the Spanish Republic.

On the other hand, we also noted with admiration how a band of valiant Englishmen laid down their lives for Spain. Even though the English had not aroused themselves sufficiently to their sense of responsibility towards China in the Far East, in their own immediate neighbourhood they did not hesitate to sacrifice themselves to the cause of freedom. Such acts of heroism reminded me over again of the true English spirit to which in those early days I had given my full faith, and made me wonder how imperialist greed could bring about so ugly a transformation in the character of so great a race.

Such is the tragic tale of the gradual loss of my faith in the claims of the European nations to civilization. In India the misfortune of being governed by a foreign race is daily brought home to us not only in the callous neglect of such minimum necessities of life as adequate provision for food, clothing, education and medical facilities for the people, but in an even unhappier form in the way people have divided themselves. The pity of it is that the blame is laid at the door of our own society. So frightful a culmination of the history of our people would never have been possible, but for the encouragement it has received from secret influences emanating from high places.

One cannot believe that Indians are in any way inferior to the Japanese in intellectual capacity. The most effective difference between these two eastern peoples is that whereas India lies at the mercy of the British, Japan has been spared the shadow of alien domination. We know what we have been deprived of. That which was truly best in their own civilizations, the upholding of the dignity of human relationships, has no place in the British administration of this country.

If in its place they have established, with baton in hand, a reign of 'law and order', in other words a policeman's rule, such mockery of civilization can claim no respect from us. It is the mission of civilization to bring unity among people and establish peace and harmony. But in unfortunate India the social fabric is being rent into shreds by unseemly outbursts of hooliganism daily growing in intensity, right under the very aegis of 'law and order'.

In India, so long as no personal injury is inflicted upon any member of the ruling race, this barbarism seems to be assured of perpetuity, making us ashamed to live under such an administration.

And yet my good fortune has often brought me into close contact with really large-hearted Englishmen. Without the slightest hesitation I may say that the nobility of their character was without parallel - in no country or community have I come across such greatness of soul. Such examples would not allow me to wholly lose faith in the race which produced them.

I had the rare blessing of having Andrews - a real Englishman, a real Christian and a true man - for a very close friend. Today in the perspective of death his unselfish and courageous magnanimity shines all the brighter. The whole of India remains indebted to him for innumerable acts of love and devotion. But personally speaking, I am especially beholden to him because he helped me to retain in my old age that feeling of respect for the English race with which in the past I was inspired by their literature and which I was about to lose completely. I count such Englishmen as Andrews not only as my personal and intimate friends but as friends of the whole human race. To have known them has been to me a treasured privilege. It is my belief that such Englishmen will save British honour from shipwreck. At any rate if I had not known them, my despair at the prospect of Western civilization would be unrelieved.

In the meanwhile the demon of barbarity has given up all pretence and has emerged with unconcealed fangs, ready to tear up humanity in an orgy of devastation. From one end of the world to the other the poisonous fumes of hatred darken the atmosphere.

The spirit of violence which perhaps lay dormant in the psychology of the West, has at last roused itself and desecrates the spirit of Man. The wheels of Fate will someday compel the English to give up their Indian empire. But what kind of India will they leave behind, what stark misery? 'When the stream of their centuries' administration runs dry at last, what a waste of mud and filth they will leave behind them! I had at one time believed that the springs of civilization would issue out of the heart of Europe. But today when I am about to quit the world that faith has gone bankrupt altogether.

As I look around I see the crumbling ruins of a proud civilization strewn like a vast heap of futility. And yet I shall not commit the grievous sin of losing faith in Man. I would rather look forward to the opening of a new chapter in his history after the cataclysm is over and the atmosphere rendered clean with the spirit of service and sacrifice. Perhaps that dawn will come from this horizon, from the East where the sun rises. A day will come when unvanquished Man will retrace his path of conquest, despite all barriers, to win back his lost human heritage.

Today we witness the perils which attend on the insolence of might; one day shall be borne out the full truth of what the sages have proclaimed: 'By unrighteousness man prospers, gains what appears desirable, conquers enemies, but perishes at the root.'

SUBHAS CHANDRA BOSE

1944

Give Me Blood and I Promise You Freedom

A leader with defiant patriotism for the country, Netaji Subhas Chandra Bose was an organizational and military leader, passionate about fighting the British to free India. He was the president of Indian National Congress from 1937-1940. His ideals bordered on extremes, believing in swaraj (self-governance) and use of force against the British. That wasn't acceptable to Mahatma Gandhi, and it led to a split in the Congress. He escaped India in 1940 and went to Germany, seeking their cooperation, believing in the proverbial, "an enemy's enemy is a friend." He is known for revamping the Indian National Army (Azad Hind Fauj), comprised mainly of Indian prisoners of war, to overthrow the British from India.

In this motivational speech presented to the Indian National Army at a rally of Indians in Burma on July 4, 1944, he proclaimed the famous slogan, 'Give me blood and I promise you freedom,' which became a national rage. His words in this speech reflect his boldness, with the element of violence and sacrifice ringing through them. Explaining about his mission of 'total mobility' in East Asia, he expressed his gratitude to the people who contributed, at the same time urging them to come forward with a daring attitude. He persuades people, ensuring them that the only way to achieve liberty would be to have maximum sacrifice in the form of martyrdom and bloodshed. He also spoke of the possibilities of defeating the British, having faith in the big Indian numbers and people, taking inspiration from brave deeds and heroic exploits.

Bose died in a plane crash over Taiwan on August 18, 1945, however since his body was never recovered, this fact is disputed.

Give Me Blood and I Promise You Freedom, 1944

Friends! Twelve months ago a new programme of 'total mobilisation' or 'maximum sacrifice' was placed before Indians in East Asia. Today I shall give you an account of our achievements during the past year and shall place before you our demands for the coming year. But, before I do so, I want you to realise once again what a golden opportunity we have for winning freedom. The British are engaged in a worldwide struggle and in the course of this struggle they have suffered defeat after defeat on so many fronts. The enemy having been thus considerably weakened, our fight for liberty has become very much easier than it was five years ago. Such a rare and God-given opportunity comes once in a century. That is why we have sworn to fully utilise this opportunity for liberating our motherland from the British yoke.

I am so very hopeful and optimistic about the outcome of our struggle, because I do not rely merely on the efforts of three million Indians in East Asia. There is a gigantic movement going on inside India and millions of our countrymen are prepared for maximum suffering and sacrifice in order to achieve liberty.

Unfortunately, ever since the great fight of 1857, our countrymen are disarmed, whereas the enemy is armed to the teeth. Without arms and without a modern army, it is impossible for a disarmed people to win freedom in this modern age.

Through the grace of Providence and through the help of generous Nippon, it has become possible for Indians in East Asia to get arms to build up a modern army. Moreover, Indians in East Asia are united to a man in the endeavour to win freedom and all the religious and other differences that the British tried to engineer inside India, simply do not exist in East Asia. Consequently, we have now an ideal combination of circumstances favouring the success of our struggle- and all that is wanted is that Indians should themselves come forward to pay the price of liberty. According to the programme of 'total mobilisation', I demanded of you men, money and materials. Regarding men, I am glad to tell you that I have obtained sufficient recruits already. Recruits have come to us from every corner of east Asia- from China, Japan, Indo-China, Philippines, Java, Borneo, Celebes, Sumatra, Malaya, Thailand and Burma.

You must continue the mobilisation of men, money and materials with greater vigour and energy, in particular, the problem of supplies and transport has to be solved satisfactorily.

We require more men and women of all categories for administration and reconstruction in liberated areas. We must be prepared for a situation in which the enemy will ruthlessly apply the scorched earth policy, before withdrawing from a particular area and will also force the civilian population to evacuate as was attempted in Burma.

The most important of all is the problem of sending reinforcements in men and in supplies to the fighting fronts. If we do not do so, we cannot hope to maintain our success at the fronts. Nor can we hope to penetrate deeper into India.

Those of you who will continue to work on the Home Front should never forget that East Asia- and particularly Burma- form our base for the war of liberation. If this base is not strong, our fighting forces can never be victorious. Remember that this is a 'total war'- and not merely a war between two armies. That is why for a full one year I have been laying so much stress on 'total mobilisation' in the East.

There is another reason why I want you to look after the Home Front properly. During the coming months I and my colleagues on the War Committee of the Cabinet desire to devote our whole attention to the fighting front- and also to the task of working up the revolution inside India. Consequently, we want to be fully assured that the work at the base will go on smoothly and uninterruptedly even in our absence.

Friends, one year ago, when I made certain demands of you, I told you that if you give me 'total mobilization', I would give you a 'second front'. I have redeemed that pledge. The first phase of our campaign is over. Our victorious troops, fighting side by side with Nipponese troops, have pushed back the enemy and are now fighting bravely on the sacred soil of our dear motherland.

Gird up your loins for the task that now lies ahead. I had asked you for men, money and materials. I have got them in generous measure. Now I demand more of you. Men, money and materials cannot by themselves bring victory or freedom. We must have the motive-power that will inspire us to brave deeds and heroic exploits.

It will be a fatal mistake for you to wish to live and see

India free simply because victory is now within reach. No one here should have the desire to live to enjoy freedom. A long fight is still in front of us.

We should have but one desire today - the desire to die so that India may live - the desire to face a martyr's death, so that the path to freedom may be paved with the martyr's blood.

Friend's! My comrades in the War of Liberation! Today I demand of you one thing, above all. I demand of you blood. It is blood alone that can avenge the blood that the enemy has spilt. It is blood alone that can pay the price of freedom.

Give me blood and I Promise you freedom.

DR. SARVEPALLI RADHAKRISHNAN

1947

Speech as First Vice-President of Independent India

Considered to be the bridge-builder between India and the west, by shaping the understanding of Hinduism, Dr. Sarvepalli Radhakrishnan is India's first Vice-President and second President from 1962-1967. He is one of India's most influential twentieth-century scholars of comparative religion and philosophy. Radhakrishnan believed that teachers should be the best minds in the country and is known to have said, "He [teacher] must himself be a fellow traveller in the exciting pursuit of knowledge". This led to the observance of Teacher's Day on September 5, his birthday, each year. He began his career with an interpretation of Rabindranath Tagore's poetry in his work, 'The Philosophy of Rabindranath Tagore'. He has been conferred with several awards, including the Bharat Ratna in 1954 and honorary membership of the British Royal Order of Merit in 1963.

As Vice-President of independent India, Dr. Radhakrishnan delivered this speech nearing midnight on August 14, 1947, at new India's dawn of independence in New Delhi. In this visionary speech, Dr. Radhakrishnan looks at India's future, believing that healing India and leading the nation would be a large battle. He spoke about the importance of cultivating unity in the face of a divide, appealing to the masses to not let differences separate them, and to have and nurture cultural and spiritual ties. India having a newly given power was also vulnerable to internal discord, and Dr. Radhakrishnan appeals to the masses, pointing out how individuals and society are even more accountable for their actions. He stresses on the importance of self-action and control in curbing evils India had been plagued with: corruption, nepotism, love of power, black marketing.

Urging people to follow those age-old ideals that have been bestowed on them, Radhakrishnan spoke of intolerance as the greatest repressor of progress and how we need to develop tolerance for others' views, thoughts and beliefs to bring about effective development.

Speech as First Vice-President of Independent India, 1947

Mr President, Sir, it is not necessary for me to speak at any great length on this Resolution so impressively moved by Pandit Jawaharlal Nehru and seconded by Mr Khaliquzzaman. History and legend will grow round this day. It marks a milestone in the march of our democracy. A significant date it is in the drama of the Indian people who are trying to rebuild and transform themselves. Through a long night of waiting, a night full of fateful portents and silent prayers for the dawn of freedom, of haunting spectres of hunger and death, our sentinels kept watch, the lights were burning bright, till at last the dawn is breaking and we greet it with the utmost enthusiasm. When we are passing from a state of serfdom, a state of slavery and subjection to one of freedom and liberation, it is an occasion for rejoicing. That it is being effected in such an orderly and dignified way, is a matter for gratification.

Mr Attlee spoke with visible pride in the House of Commons when he said that this is the first great instance of a strong Imperialist power transferring its authority to a subject people whom it ruled with force and firmness for nearly two centuries. For a parallel, he cited the British withdrawal from South Africa; but it is nothing comparable in scale and circumstances to the British withdrawal from this country. When we see what the Dutch are doing in Indonesia, when we see how the French are clinging to their possessions, we cannot but admire the political sagacity and courage of the British people.

We on our side have also added a chapter to the history of the World. Look at the way in which subject peoples in history won their freedom. Let us also consider the methods by which power was acquired. How did men like Washington, Napoleon, Cromwell, Lenin, Hitler and Mussolini get into power? Look at the methods of blood and steel, of terrorism and assassination, of bloodshed and anarchy by which these so-called great-men of the world came into the possession of power. Here in this land under the leadership of one who will go down in history as perhaps the greatest man of our age, we have opposed patience to fury, quietness of spirit to bureaucratic tyranny and are acquiring power through peaceful and civilised methods. What is the result? The transition is being effected with the least bitterness, with utterly no kind of hatred at all. The very fact that we are appointing Lord Mountbatten as the Governor-General of India shows the spirit of understanding and friendliness in which this whole transition is being effected.

You, Mr President, referred to the sadness in our hearts, to the sorrow which also clouds our rejoicings. May I say that we are in an essential sense responsible for it also, though not entirely. From 1600, Englishmen have come to this country - priests and nuns, merchants and adventurers, diplomats and statesmen, missionaries and idealists. They bought and sold, marched and fought, plotted and profited, helped and healed. The greatest among them wished to modernise the country, to raise its intellectual and moral standards, its political status. They wished to regenerate the whole people. But the small among them worked with sinister objective. They tried to increase the disunion in the country, made the country poorer, weaker and more disunited. They also have had their chance now.

The freedom we are attaining is the fulfilment of this dual tendency among British administrators. While India is attaining freedom, she is attaining it in a manner which does not produce joy in the hearts of people or a radiant smile on their faces. Some of those who were charged with the responsibility for the administration of this country, tried to accentuate communal consciousness and bring about the present result which is a logical outcome of the policies adopted by the lesser minds of Britain. But I would never blame them. Were we not victims, ready victims, so to say, of the separatist tendencies foisted on us? Should we not now correct our national faults of character, our domestic despotism, our intolerance which has assumed the different forms of obscurantism of narrow-mindedness, of superstitious bigotry?

Others were able to play on our weakness because we had them. I would like therefore to take this opportunity to call for self examination, for a searching of hearts. We have gained but we have not gained in the manner we wished to gain and if we have not done so, the responsibility is our own. And when this pledge says that we have to serve our country, we can best serve our country by removing these fundamental defects which have prevented us from gaining the objective of a free and united India.

Now that India is divided, it is our duty not to indulge in words of anger. They lead us nowhere. We must avoid passion. Passion and wisdom never go together. The body politic may be divided but the body historic lives on.

Political divisions, physical partitions, are external but the psychological divisions are deeper. The cultural cleavages are the more dangerous. We should not allow them to grow. What we should do is to preserve those cultural ties, those spiritual bonds which knit our peoples together into one organic whole.

Patient consideration, slow process of education, adjustment to one another's needs, the discovery of points of view which are common to both the dominions in the matter of Communications, Defence, Foreign Affairs; these are the things which should be allowed to grow in the daily business of life and administration. It is by developing such attitudes that we can once again draw near and gain the lost unity of this country. That is the only way to it.

Our opportunities are great but let me warn you that when power outstrips ability, we will fall on evil days. We should develop competence and ability which would help us to utilise the opportunities which are now open to us. From tomorrow morning - from midnight today - we cannot throw the blame on the Britisher. We have to assume the responsibility ourselves for what we do. A free India will be judged by the way in which it will serve the interests of the common man in the matter of food, clothing, shelter and the social services.

Unless we destroy corruption in high places, root out every trace of nepotism, love of power, profiteering and black marketing which have spoiled the good name of this great country in recent times, we will not be able to raise the standards of efficiency in administration as well as in the production and distribution of the necessary goods of life.

Pandit Jawaharlal Nehru referred to the great contribution which this country will make to the promotion of world peace and the welfare at mankind. The chakra, the Asokan wheel, which is there in the flag, embodies for us a great idea, Asoka, the greatest of our emperors. Look at the words of H.G. Wells regarding him, 'Highnesses, Magnificence's, Excellences, Serenities, Majesties;' among them all, he shines alone a star Asoka, the greatest of all monarchs.' He cut into rock his message for the healing of discords. If there are differences, the way in which you can solve them is by promoting concord. Concord is the only way by which we can get rid of differences. There is no other method which is open to us.

We are lucky in having for our leader one who is a world citizen, who is essentially a humanist, who possesses a buoyant optimism and robust good sense in spite of the perversity of things and the hostility of human affairs. We see the way in which his Department interfered actively and in a timely manner in the Indonesian dispute. It shows that if India gains freedom, that freedom will be used not merely for the well-being of India but for Vishva Kalyana, world peace, the welfare of mankind.

Our pledge tells us that this ancient land shall attain her rightful and honoured place. We take pride in the antiquity of this land for it is a land which has been nearly four or five millenniums of history. It has passed through many vicissitudes and at the moment it stands, still responding to the thrill of the same great ideal.

Civilisation is a thing of the spirit. It is not something external, solid and mechanical. It is the dream in the people's hearts. It is the inward aspiration of the people's souls. It is the imaginative interpretation of the human life and the perception of the mystery of human existence. That is what civilisation actually stands for.

We should bear in mind these great ideals which have been transmitted to us across the ages. In this great time of our history we should bear ourselves humbly before God, brace ourselves to this supreme task which is confronting us and conduct ourselves in a manner that is worthy of the ageless spirit of India.

If we do so, I have no doubt that the future of this land will be as great as its once-glorious past.

Sarvabhutdisahamatmanam
Sarvabhutani catmani
Sampasyam atmayajivai
Saarwjyam adhigachati

Swarajya is the development of that kind of tolerant attitude which sees in brother man, the face Divine. Intolerance has been the greatest enemy of our progress. Tolerance of one another's views, thoughts and beliefs is the only remedy that we can possibly adopt.

Therefore I support with very great pleasure this Resolution which asks us as the representatives of the people of India to conduct ourselves in all humility in the service of our country. The word 'Humility' here means that we are by ourselves very insignificant. Our efforts by themselves cannot carry us to a long distance.

We should make ourselves dependent on that other than ourselves which makes for righteousness. The note of humility means the unimportance of the individual and the supreme importance of the unfolding purpose which we are called upon to serve. So in a mood of humility, in a spirit of dedication let us take this pledge as soon as the clock strikes twelve.

PANDIT JAWAHARLAL NEHRU

1947

Tryst with Destiny

The architect of the modern Indian nation as a sovereign, socialist, secular, and democratic republic, Pandit Jawaharlal Nehru was a central figure in Indian politics and an important leader in the Indian independence movement. When the negotiations between Nehru and Muhammad Ali Jinnah, leader of the Muslim League failed, it gave way to the partition of India in 1947.

On the eve of India's independence, nearing midnight on August 14, 1947, Jawaharlal Nehru, independent India's first Prime Minister, made this historic speech to the Constituent Assembly of India in New Delhi. Tryst with destiny is considered to be one of the greatest speeches of all time, being a verbal milestone announcing India's freedom from the British colonial rule after a long struggle.

In this carefully drafted speech, Pandit Nehru revelled in the fact that India had finally come to that hour of freedom, with which it had made a tryst, and which had been pledged by Indians years before. With his powerful words, he urged Indians to be strong and ambitious, instilling hope in every heart that had suffered. He spoke of responsibility that came along with freedom and power, implying how India would have to strive hard to become less dependent on other countries. As a new beginning for the whole country, in the morning of August 15, he was officially sworn in as the first Prime Minister of independent India.

Rejoicing in the new dawn for India, Pandit Nehru visualized a bright future for the country, where the people would strive hard to achieve what they are capable of, making India a model nation for the rest. He also foresaw the new destiny for India as being able to alleviate poverty, disease, ignorance and having equal opportunities for all.

Long years ago we made a tryst with destiny, and now the time comes when we shall redeem our pledge, not wholly or in full measure, but very substantially. At the stroke of the midnight hour, when the world sleeps, India will awake to life and freedom.

A moment comes, which comes but rarely in history, when we step out from the old to the new, when an age ends, and when the soul of a nation, long suppressed, finds utterance. It is fitting that at this solemn moment, we take the pledge of dedication to the service of India and her people and to the still larger cause of humanity. At the dawn of history, India started on her unending quest, and trackless centuries are filled with her striving and grandeur of her success and failures. Through good and ill fortune alike, she has never lost sight of that quest, forgotten the ideals which gave her strength.

We end today a period of misfortunes and India discovers herself again. The achievement we celebrate today is but a step, an opening of opportunity to the greater triumphs and achievements that await us. Are we brave enough and wise enough to grasp this opportunity and accept the challenge of the future?

Freedom and power bring responsibility. The responsibility rests upon this Assembly, a sovereign body representing the sovereign people of India. Before the birth of freedom, we have endured all the pains of labour and our hearts are heavy with the memory of this sorrow. Some of those pains continue even now. Nevertheless, the past is over and it is the future that beckons us now.

That future is not one of ease or resting but of incessant striving so that we may fulfill the pledges we have so often taken and the one we shall take today. The service of India means the service of the millions who suffer. It means the ending of poverty and ignorance and poverty and disease and inequality of opportunity. The ambition of the greatest men of our generation has been to wipe every tear from every eye. That may be beyond us, but as long as there are tears and suffering, so long our work will not be over.

And so we have to labour and to work, and to work hard, to give reality to our dreams. Those dreams are for India, but they are also for the world, for all the nations and peoples are too closely knit together today for any one of them to imagine that it can live apart. Peace is said to be indivisible, so is freedom, so is prosperity now, and also is disaster in this one world that can no longer be split into isolated fragments.

To the people of India, whose representatives we are, we make an appeal to join us with faith and confidence in this great adventure. This is no time for petty and destructive criticism, no time for ill-will or blaming others. We have to build the noble mansion of free India where all her children may dwell.

The appointed day has come -the day appointed by destiny- and India stands forth again, after long slumber and struggle, awake, vital, free and independent. The past clings on to us still in some measure and we have to do much before we redeem the pledges we have so often taken. Yet the turning-point is past, and history begins anew for us, the history which we shall live and act and others will write about.

It is a fateful moment for us in India, for all Asia and for the world. A new star rises, the star of freedom in the East, a new hope comes into being, a vision long cherished materializes. May the star never set and that hope never betrayed!

We rejoice in that freedom, even though clouds surround us, and many of our people are sorrow-stricken and difficult problems encompass us. But freedom brings responsibilities and burdens and we have to face them in the spirit of a free and disciplined people. On this day our first thoughts go to the architect of this freedom, the Father of our Nation, who, embodying the old spirit of India, held aloft the torch of freedom and lighted up the darkness that surrounded us.

We have often been unworthy followers of his and have strayed from his message, but not only we but succeeding generations will remember this message and bear the imprint in their hearts of this great son of India, magnificent in his faith and strength and courage and humility. We shall never allow that torch of freedom to be blown out, however high the wind or stormy the tempest. Our next thoughts must be of the unknown volunteers and soldiers of freedom who, without praise or reward, have served India even unto death.

We think also of our brothers and sisters who have been cut off from us by political boundaries and who unhappily cannot share at present in the freedom that has come. They are of us and will remain of us whatever may happen, and we shall be sharers in their good [or] ill fortune alike.

The future beckons to us. Whither do we go and what shall be our endeavour? To bring freedom and opportunity to the common man, to the peasants and workers of India; to fight and end poverty and ignorance and disease; to build up a prosperous, democratic and progressive nation, and to create social, economic and political institutions which will ensure justice and fullness of life to every man and woman.

We have hard work ahead. There is no resting for any one of us till we redeem our pledge in full, till we make all the people of India what destiny intended them to be. We are citizens of a great country on the verge of bold advance, and we have to live up to that high standard. All of us, to whatever religion we may belong, are equally the children of India with equal rights, privileges and obligations. We cannot encourage communalism or narrow-mindedness, for no nation can be great whose people are narrow in thought or in action.

To the nations and peoples of the world we send greetings and pledge ourselves to cooperate with them in furthering peace, freedom and democracy. And to India, our much-loved motherland, the ancient, the eternal and the ever-new, we pay our reverent homage and we bind ourselves afresh to her service.

Jai Hind.

SARDAR VALLABHBHAI PATEL

1948

Speech at Calcutta Maidan

One of the founding fathers of Republic of India, Vallabhbhai Patel was conferred the sobriquet 'Iron Man of India' for his fierce nationalism and able leadership. He played a crucial role in resolving the issue of more than five hundred self-governed princely states in India after independence with wisdom and diplomacy. Vallabhbhai Patel is credited for effectively guiding the country in its integration into a united nation. Always at the forefront of rebellions and political events, this notable personality was called 'Sardar', meaning 'Chief' in Hindi, Urdu and Persian.

He was a lawyer by profession, but he gave up his lucrative legal practice to join Mahatma Gandhi, by whom he was immensely influenced, in his relief work for peasants in Gujarat. He was an ardent supporter of Gandhi's non-cooperation movement and helped organize a network of volunteers to work with different villages. Quickly rising through the ranks, he was an important member of the Indian National Congress and became the first Home Minister and Deputy Prime Minister for India. He also established the modern all-India services and is called the 'Patron Saint' of India's civil servants.

In this straightforward speech delivered to thousands of

Indians gathered at the Calcutta Maidan on January 3, 1948, Patel raises the issue of Pakistan wanting to claim Junagarh as part of their country. He draws references to Kashmir and the unrest in the state, warning Pakistan to not misuse their resources or to deceive India in any way. Patel also warns the country against any serious talk of a Hindu state, as India had elected to be secular. This is a translated excerpt from the complete speech.

When I came here yesterday, I read in the newspaper that Zaffarulla Sahib proposed to include Junagarh in Pakistan. All that talk is fine, but the consequences will ultimately be borne by the Nawab of Junagarh, not Zaffarulla Sahib. All this is empty talk. You can go to the UNO, you can traverse the world, but you can't undo what's been done. Zafarullah Sahab has been threatening us, saying that even Junagarh would go to UNO and demand special status. They can for all we care. Even Kashmir went to the UNO and we are fine with it. Pakistan should fight its war openly rather than using Kashmir to serve their propaganda. They supply Kashmir with arms and men and influence them to fight Pakistan's wars.

India also cannot stay silent. I reiterate that Kashmir is a different matter. Junagarh cannot go to UNO simply because it came to us of its own accord. We didn't influence it in any way; neither through arms nor money nor promises. Junagarh's Diwan came to us and pleaded to be a part of the Republic of India. And we accepted.

We have decided that from now on we should leave the choice of realms to people and act on public consensus. We don't mind if states govern themselves according to people's consent. Kashmir can do the same. But we can't let Kashmir continue in its present state of violence and unrest. If Pakistan wants to establish their foothold over Kashmir by force, where is the scope for democracy? We still favour a representative government but if Pakistan keeps on with the killings of our policemen using our money, burning our villages and massacring our Hindus and Sikhs, then that's not democracy. Then we will also have to pick up arms. You haven't left us a choice.

But let me be clear on one point. We aren't going to give up Kashmir. Not now. Not ever. Another thing you have to understand is that you should not force our hand when we are in such a delicate situation. Now that India, along with the world is in a fragile situation, what is the right way forward? We should co-operate with our government and leaders because if we don't we will be in much worse position. Lakhs of people have gathered here in Calcutta today, and I want to sincerely appeal to you to take this message forward to your fellow Indians. You should tell them that the need of the hour is to stay united and work in harmony with each other, to support our leaders.

Everyone says that they want a secular state and not one dominated and ruled by Hindus. But what I say is, it is not possible for there to be a state governed by Hindus, as there are about 3-4 crore Muslims in India. Another thing that I would like to being to your attention is that the same Muslims advocated for a separate country: Pakistan. What I don't understand, is how can their minds change overnight and their loyalties altered? Now that they declare loyalty to us, and question us on our suspicions of Muslims, we say why question us? You should look within yourself and ask the same question.

You asked for Pakistan and you got it. But please don't come to us when you are in a rut. Many people wish for Pakistan and India to unite and become a single realm, but I implore them to not speak of it and let things be. This is a risky proposition. Let Pakistan develop; let it become good as heaven. Make it strong and make it robust. We as neighbours, stand to benefit from it.

Too many times has it been suggested that we have conspired against Pakistan. To Pakistan's leaders I would say that all their enemies, all the conspiracies take root within Pakistan. They don't have enemies outside their own borders. We wish you well, we always have. We let you carve Pakistan out of our own land. But if you deceive us, we won't tolerate it. Stay out of our country, our governance and our matters; and we won't interfere in yours. We have shown generosity and given you more than your fair share of resources. But when it came to money, we said that if you want your 1600 crores, we are ready to give that to you and more. But I have given it in writing that if you use this money to fuel riots in Kashmir, you won't get any money from us. If you have it in you, come and claim it from us. We will give the money happily once it's proved that it is yours. We have a decree of consent which will be honoured after the matter of Kashmir is decided in the court of law. But they accuse us of intentionally withholding money. Had our intentions been wrong, why would we have consented to the decree in the first place? We don't conduct ourselves in this manner. I want to emphasize this again and again that neither do we do have animosity towards them, nor do we want to build it. They should live and let live. Let us be.

PANDIT DEENDAYAL UPADHYAYA

1965

Lecture on Integral Humanism

Pandit Deendayal Upadhyaya was an esteemed Indian sociologist, economist, philosopher, historian and political activist. One of the most important leaders of the Bharatiya Jana Sangh, the forerunner of the present day Bharatiya Janata Party, he is credited with coming up with the concept of Integral Humanism, an indigenous economic model that puts the human being at centre stage. He is known to have always maintained the highest standards of personal integrity. His concepts and ideologies became a guiding force for an alternative model of governance and politics, and are followed by his faithful followers even now. He has been the source of ideological guidance and moral inspiration for the BJP since its inception.

Pandit Deendayal Upadhyaya delivered a speech on 'Integral Humanism' in a series of lectures in Bombay. In this lecture delivered on the first day, April 22, 1965, Pandit Deendayal Upadhyaya begins explaining the concept of Integral Humanism, which he supported and propagated wholeheartedly. Drawing parallels with socio-political concepts adopted by the western world, Pandit Deendayal Upadhyaya reflect upon the situation in our nation after nearly two decades of independence. He explains the Marxist theory of capitalism giving way to socialism, why it is ideal and how Indians should view it.

He also addresses the burning questions related to progress of the nation, talking about the role played by political parties in the Indian scenario. In the midst of all this, Pandit Deendayal Upadhyaya created a thought-base to help us understand the underlying reasons, theories and thoughts behind the concept of Integral Communism.

I am asked to present my thoughts on the subject of "Integral Humanism" in a series of talks beginning this evening. Last January at Vijayavada, Bharatiya Jana Sangh adopted the statement of "Principles & Policies" in which 'Integral Humanism' has also been accepted. There have been scattered discussions here and there on the subject. It is necessary that we consider Integral Humanism in all its aspects. So long as the country was under the yoke of the British rule, all the movements and policies in the country had one principle - 'aim to drive out the foreign rulers and to achieve independence'. But what would be the face of the new Bharat after independence? In which direction were we to advance? These questions were precisely thought out. It would not be correct to say that no thought was devoted to these aspects. There were people who even at that time had considered these questions. Gandhiji himself had set out his idea of the independent Bharat in his book "Hind Swaraj". Prior to this, Lokmanya Tilak discussed the philosophical basis of the rejuvenation of Bharat in his book 'Gita Rahasya'. He gave a comparative discussion of various schools of thought all over the world at that time.

Apart from these, the Congress and other political parties adopted various resolutions from time to time which contain references to this subject. However, the subject requires much more serious study than was devoted to it at that time. It did not attract serious attention at that time because everyone believed it was more important to think of ways to drive out the British and the other things could be discussed later on. It did not seem right to waste time in internal discussions while the foreign rule continued. Hence even if there might have been difference in views, they were shelved for the time being.

As a result, even those who held the view that socialism should be the basis of the future Bharat, worked inside the Congress as a socialist group. They did attempt to form as a separate party as such. The revolutionaries too, were working independence in their own way. All agreed, however, that the foremost task was to gain independence.

Having attained independence, the question naturally ought to have occurred to us, "Now that we independent, what shall be the direction of our progress?" But it is amazing that serious thought has not been given to this question and today even after seventeen years' independence, we cannot say that a definite direction been decided upon.

Whither Bharat

From time to time, Congressmen or others have declared Welfare State, Socialism, Liberalism etc. as their aims. Slogans have been raised. But this ideology attached little significance to the philosophies, apart from the slogans. I am saying this on the basis of personal discussions. A leading gentleman once suggested during a conversation that a joint front should be against Congress, whereby a good fight can be given. Now a days, political parties adopt this strategy. So it was surprising to put forward this suggestion. However, naturally, I asked, "What programme shall we adopt? If such a joint front is formed some idea of the programme is essential. What will be our economic policy? What will our foreign policy? These questions should also be broadly tackled."

"Do not worry about it. Whatever you like you can adopt. We are ready to support anything from extreme Marxist to downright capitalist program." The reply came as if this was natural. He had no difficulty in adopting any programme. The only object was that somehow Congress should be defeated. Even now some declare that Congress must be defeated even with the cooperation of communists and all the rest.

Recently elections were held in Kerala. During the elections, Communists, Muslim League, Swatantra Party, S.S.P. Rebel Congress known as Kerala Congress, Revolutionary Socialist Party etc. entered into a variety of bilateral of multiple alliances. As a result, it was difficult to imagine that any of these parties had a definite ideology, principles and aims. This is the situation as far as principles are concerned.

Congress too, is in a similar state. Even though the Congress has proclaimed democratic socialism as its goal, the behaviour of various Congress leaders shows one thing clearly that there are no definite principles, no single direction in Congress. There are staunch communists in Congress fold. There are also those who have faith in capitalism and oppose communism to the teeth. All brands of people are arrayed on Congress platform. If there can be a magic box which contains a cobra and a mongoose living together, it is Congress.

We must ponder whether we can progress under such conditions. If we stop to analyze the reasons for the problems facing the country, we will find that the confusion about our goal and the direction is mainly responsible for the chaos. I realize that all the 450 million people of Bharat cannot agree on all or even on a single question. That is not possible in any country. Yet there is generally, what is called a more or less common desire of the people of any nation. If this popular longing is made the basis of our aims, the common man feels that the nation is moving in a proper direction, and that his own aspiration is reflected in the efforts of the nation. This also generates the greatest possible feeling of unity. The truth of the statement is borne out by the response of the people during the Chinese Invasion of October/November 1962. A wave of enthusiasm swept across the country. Action and sacrifice both obtained in abundance. There was no barrier between the government and the public or between various political parties. How did this happen? The external threat made us recognize ourselves. The government adopted that policy which reflected the widespread feeling in the people and which enhanced their sense of self-respect with a call for sacrifice. The result was that we stood united.

The Root of Our Problems - Neglect of Self

It is essential that we think about our national identity. Without this identity there is no meaning. Independence neither means anything, nor can independence become the instrument of progress and happiness. As long as we are unaware of our national identity, we cannot recognize and develop all our potentialities. Under alien rule this identity is suppressed. That is why nations wish to remain independent so that they can progress according to their natural bent and can experience happiness in their endeavour. Nature is powerful.

An attempt to go against nature or to disregard her, leads to troubles. The natural instincts cannot be disregarded but it is possible to elevate this nature to the level of culture. Psychology informs us how by suppression of various natural instincts, different mental disorders ensue. Such a person remains restless and dejected. His abilities slowly deteriorate and become perverted. The Nation too like the individual becomes prey to numerous ills when its natural instincts are disregarded. The basic cause of the problems facing Bharat is the neglect of its national identity.

Opportunism Has Shaken the Confidence of People in Politics

A majority of those who lead the nation today as well as those who take active interest in the affairs of the country are not sufficiently aware of this root cause. Consequently opportunists with no principles reign in politics of our country. Parties and politicians have neither principles nor aims nor a standard code of conduct. A person feels nothing wrong in leaving one party and joining another. Even alliances and mergers of parties or their bifurcations are dictated not by agreement or by differences in principles but purely by gains in elections or in positions of power. In 1939 Shri Hafiz Mohammed Ibrahim was elected the Muslim League ticket. Later when he joined Congress, in accordance with healthy principles of public conduct, he resigned and sought re-election on Congress ticket and was once again elected. In 1948 when socialists left Congress and founded Socialist Party, all those who were members of legislature resigned and fought elections on socialist tickets. But thereafter this healthy tradition was forgotten. Now there is complete license in politics. As result, in the public's mind there is distrust for everyone. There is hardly any reason or person whose integrity is beyond doubt in the public mind. This situation must be changed.

What Should Be Our Direction?

The nation is at crossroads. Some people suggest that we must start from where we have left off one thousand years ago, when foreign invaders disrupted our life. But nation is not an inanimate object like a cloth that allows weaving to be taken up after a gap in time. Besides it would not be rational to say that the thousand year old alien rule has interrupted the current of our national life so completely that from that time to this day we remained stationary and inactive. The nation has certainly put her genius to work, in the changing circumstances to meet the challenges thrown at her. We have struggled to continue our life forward and to wrest independence from the aliens. The current of our national life was not interrupted but has gone on ceaselessly. The task of turning the waters of Ganga back to some previous point would not be wise. Ganga at Banaras may not be crystal clear as at Haridwar. But still it is the same holy Ganga. It has absorbed numerous rivulets with all their refuse. However, these have no separate existence but have become Ganga. The current Ganga must inevitably grow onwards. If this was all that happened, it would still not be a big problem. But there are other nations in the world. They have made phenomenal progress in the past one thousand years. Our entire attention was engaged in fighting for independence or staving off new hordes of invaders. We have not been able to contribute to the world progress. Now when we are free, is it not paramount that we fill this deficiency at the earliest and stand shoulder to shoulder with other advanced nations of the world?

Up to this point there is no room for difference of opinion. The difficulty arises when we fail to discern the reasons for the spectacular advance of the West, its effects, real and apparent. This is further complicated by the fact that Britishers were a representative of the West, ruled this country for a century and, during this period adopted such measures whereby in the minds of our people, a contempt for things Bharatiya and respect for everything Western were subtly created. Along with scientific advancement, their way of life, manners and food habits etc. came to this country. Not only material sciences but also their social, economic and political doctrines became our standards. Today the educated in this country clearly display this effect. We shall have to decide whether this effect is good or bad for us. We had taken pride in resisting things British while they ruled us, but strangely enough, now that the Britishers have left, westernisation has become synonymous with progress. It is true that a narrow sense of nationalism should not be allowed to obstruct the progress of the nation. However, western science and the western way of life are two different things. While western science is universal and must be absorbed by us if we wish to go forward, the same is not true about the western way of life and values. In fact, thoughtless imitation of the West must be scrupulously discarded. There are those who consider economic and political doctrines of the West as epitome of progress and desire to transplant the same in our country. Therefore when we are trying to decide where wish to take our country and how, we must also take into consideration the basis of various economic and political doctrines of the west and their present position.

The Rise of European Nations

Among various Isms that affected the West, the principal ones are Nationalism, Democracy and Socialism. At the same time there have been some who cherish world unity and world peace and have made some efforts in that direction.

Among these, nationalism is the oldest and the strongest. After the fall of the Roman Empire and decline in the influence of the Catholic Church, Europe witnessed rise of several nations. History of Europe in the past thousand years is the history of the rise of and conflict among various nations. These nations extended their empires beyond the European continent and subjugated other independent countries. Nationalism brought nation and state together resulting in nation states. At the same time the decline in the influence of the Roman Catholic Church gave rise either to national churches or to complete disappearance of religious influence on politics. Anyway the concept of secular state arose out of this situation.

Birth of Democracy in Europe

A revolutionary concept which made a deep impact on the political life of Europe is Democracy. In the beginning, every nation had a king as its head but there was gradual awakening in the minds of people against the autocracy of the royalty. The industrial revolution and the international trade resulted in the rise of a business community in all nations. Naturally there ensued a conflict between these new centres of power and the established kings and feudal lords. This conflict adopted 'democracy' as its philosophical basis. The origin of democracy was sought in the Greek city republics. The common man was attracted by the lofty ideals of equality, fraternity and liberty of every citizen. France witnessed a bloody revolution. In England too, there were periodic movements. The idea of democracy gained foothold in the mind of common man. The royalty was either liquidated or their powers were drastically curbed and constitutional governments were established. Today democracy has been already accepted in Europe. Even those who have suppressed democracy do not denounce it. The dictators like Hitler, Mussolini and Stalin too paid lip service to democracy.

Individual Was Exploited

Every individual got a vote in the democratic setup. But real power stayed with those who had led the revolution. Industrial revolution had generated faith in the new methods of production. Instead of working in the freedom of home, workers had started working in the factories taking orders from the factory owners, the worker migrated from his home town to dwell in crowded cities. There was no provision of proper housing. There were hardly any rules in the factory to protect the worker. He was economically weak and not yet organized. He became a victim of exploitation, injustice and harassment. Those in whom political power was vested were members of the same group who exploited the workers. Hence there was no hope of redress from the state.

A number of persons led movements in protest against this injustice with the desire to improve the lot of workers. They called themselves socialists. Karl Marx was one of them. In an effort to lead the movement against t injustice, he studied the entire history and structure, and presented his analysis of the situation. He claimed to have given a scientific basis to his theories. All the subsequent socialists might not have agreed with Marx but they all were considerably influenced by his ideas.

Dictatorship of the Proletariat

According to Marx's analysis-dialectic materialism, the root cause of exploitation lies in the private owners of the means of production. If these means are made the property of the society (for the Marxist, the Society is synonymous with the State) then there will be no further exploitation. But before this, the state should be redeemed from the hands of the exploiters and ensured against their influence in future. Towards this end, dictatorship of proletariat must be established. In order that people tolerate this dictatorship, it was held as an ideal that when the exploiter class has been finally liquidated, and possibility of its resurgence exists, the state will be replaced by a classless, stateless society. Marx also attempted to show that capitalism contains seeds of its own destruction and that socialism is inevitable.

In some countries of Europe, there was social revolution. Even where socialism was not accepted, politicians had to accept the rights of workers. "Welfare State" was accepted as an ideal. Nationalism, democracy, socialism or equality (equality is there at the root of socialism; equality is different from equability), these three doctrines have dominated European social political thinking. Every now and then apart from these, ideals of world peace and world unity also cropped up. All these are good ideas. They reflect the higher aspirations mankind. But by itself each of these doctrines is incomplete. Not only that, each stands opposed to the rest in practice. Nationalism poses a threat to world peace. Democracy and capitalism join hands to give a free reign to exploitation. Socialism replaced capitalism and brought with it democracy and individual freedom. Hence the West is faced with the task of reconciling these good ideals. They have not succeeded to this day, in this task. They have tried combinations and permutations, by emphasis on one or the other ideal. England emphasized nationalism and democracy and developed her politico-social institutions along those lines, whereas France could not adopt the same. There, democracy resulted in political instability.

The British Labour party wanted to reconcile socialism with democracy but people have raised doubts whether democracy will survive if socialism gains strength. Hence the labour party no longer supports socialism as strongly as the Marxist doctrines advocate. If socialism has been diluted considerably, it is because Hitler and Mussolini adopted nationalist cum socialism and buried democracy. In the end socialism also became a tool for their nationalism which posed a great threat to world peace and unity. We may indeed seek some guidance from the western world but the fact is that it has no concrete suggestions to offer. It is itself at crossroads unable to decide what is good. Under such circumstances, we cannot expect guidance from the West. On the contrary we must consider whether in this present state of the world, we can contribute something to resolve its dilemma. Having taken note of the progress of the world, can we add to the common store of knowledge? As a member of the world community, we must discharge our responsibilities. If we possess something that may prove helpful to world progress, we should not hesitate in imparting it to the world. In this era of adulteration, instead of adulterating ideas we must on the contrary scrutinize and improve upon them wherever possible before accepting them. Rather than being a burden on the world, we must attempt to resolve the problems facing the world.

We must also consider what contribution our tradition and civilization make to the world culture. We shall consider this tomorrow evening.

MOTHER TERESA

1979

Nobel Peace Prize Acceptance

Mother Teresa (born Agnes Gonxha Bojaxhiu in Skopje, Macedonia, on August 26, 1910) was felicitated with the Nobel Peace Prize on December 10, 1979 in Oslo, Norway. She was awarded for her work in 'bringing help to suffering humanity', and had dedicated her life to the sick and hungry. She wanted to spread the message: "the poor must know that we love them". She travelled to India, where from 1931 to 1948 she taught at St. Mary's High School, before deciding to dedicate herself to the poorest of the poor in the slums of Calcutta. With her efforts, thousands of sick and dying poor were provided shelter and treatment, and children cared for and provided foster homes.

She founded The Missionaries of Charity in 1950, which grew up to be a world-wide organization, now providing shelter and effective help to the poor in Asia, Europe, Africa, Latin America and Australia. They also undertake relief work during natural calamities, and the houses in North America, Europe and Australia take care of alcoholics, AIDS sufferers and the homeless.

In her humble acceptance speech for the Nobel Prize,

Mother Teresa spoke of 'love' as a great power, and how she believes it is love that people, especially the poorest of the poor, need. She provided heart-warming instances from her life and people she came across and how she learned something from each of them. Mother Teresa believed that abortion is the highest form of evil, as it is the killing of a life that has already been conceived. To reduce numbers in abortion, her charity encouraged women to give birth, with the baby being adopted into a home where they're wanted. Her stand against abortion and focus on natural family planning drew some amount of criticism, but she nevertheless stood by her beliefs and was widely regarded as a saint and a blessing for the poor. She left for her heavenly abode on September 5, 1997 in Kolkata.

Nobel Peace Prize Acceptance, 1979

As we have gathered here together to thank God for the Nobel Peace Prize, I think it will be beautiful that we pray the prayer of St. Francis of Assisi which always surprises me very much. We pray this prayer every day after Holy Communion, because it is very fitting for each one of us, and I always wonder that 400 - 500 years ago as St. Francis of Assisi composed this prayer that they had the same difficulties that we have today, as we compose this prayer that fits very nicely for us also. I think some of you already have got it, so we will pray together.

> Lord, make me a channel of Thy peace that, where there is hatred, I may bring love;
>
> That, where there is wrong, I may bring the spirit of forgiveness;
>
> That, where there is discord, I may bring harmony;
>
> That, where there is error, I may bring truth;
>
> That, where there is doubt, I may bring faith;
>
> That, where there is despair, I may bring hope;
>
> That, where there are shadows, I may bring light;

That, where there is sadness, I may bring joy.

Lord, grant that I may seek rather to comfort than to be comforted, to understand than to be understood; to love than to be loved; for it is by forgetting self that one finds; it is forgiving that one is forgiven; it is by dying that one awakens to eternal life.

Let us thank God for the opportunity that we all have together today, for this gift of peace that reminds us that we have been created to live that peace, and Jesus became man to bring that good news to the poor. He being God, became man in all things like us except sin, and he proclaimed very clearly that he had come to give the good news. The news was peace to all of good will and this is something that we all want - the peace of heart - and God loved the world so much that he gave his son - it was a giving - it is as much as if to say it hurt God to give, because he loved the world so much that he gave his son, and he gave him to Virgin Mary, and what did she do with him?

As soon as he came in her life - immediately she went in haste to give that good news, and as she came into the house of her cousin, the child - the unborn child - the child in the womb of Elizabeth, leapt with joy. He was that little unborn child, was the first messenger of peace. He recognised the Prince of Peace, he recognised that Christ has come to bring the good news for you and for me. And as if that was not enough - it was not enough to become a man - he died on the cross to show that greater love, and he died for you and for me and for that leper and for that man dying of hunger and that naked person lying in the street not only of Calcutta, but of Africa, and New

York, and London, and Oslo - and insisted that we love one another as he loves each one of us. And we read that in the Gospel very clearly - love as I have loved you - as I love you - as the Father has loved me, I love you - and the harder the Father loved him, he gave him to us, and how much we love one another, we, too, must give each other until it hurts.

It is not enough for us to say: I love God, but I do not love my neighbour. St. John says you are a liar if you say you love God and you don't love your neighbour. How can you love God whom you do not see, if you do not love your neighbour whom you see, whom you touch, with whom you live. And so this is very important for us to realise that love, to be true, has to hurt. It hurt Jesus to love us, it hurt him. And to make sure we remember his great love, he made himself the bread of life to satisfy our hunger for his love. Our hunger for God, because we have been created for that love. We have been created in his image. We have been created to love and be loved, and then he has become man to make it possible for us to love as he loved us. He makes himself the hungry one - the naked one - the homeless one - the sick one - the one in prison - the lonely one - the unwanted one - and he says: You did it to me. Hungry for our love, and this is the hunger of our poor people. This is the hunger that you and I must find, it may be in our own home.

I never forget an opportunity I had in visiting a home where they had all these old parents of sons and daughters who had just put them in an institution and forgotten maybe. And I went there, and I saw in that home they had everything, beautiful things, but everybody was looking towards the door. And I did not see a single one with a smile on their face. And I turned to the Sister and I asked: How is that? How is it that the people they have everything here, why are they all looking towards the door, why are they not smiling? I am so used to see the smile on our people, even the dying one smile, and she said: This is nearly every day, they are expecting, they are hoping that a son or daughter will come to visit them. They are hurt because they are forgotten, and see - this is where love comes. That poverty comes right there in our own home, even neglect to love. Maybe in our own family we have somebody who is feeling lonely, who is feeling sick, who is feeling worried, and these are difficult days for everybody. Are we there, are we there to receive them, is the mother there to receive the child?

I was surprised in the West to see so many young boys and girls given into drugs, and I tried to find out why - why is it like that, and the answer was: Because there is no one in the family to receive them. Father and mother are so busy, they have no time. Young parents are in some institution and the child takes back to the street and gets involved in something. We are talking of peace. These are things that break peace, but I feel the greatest destroyer of peace today is abortion, because it is a direct war, a direct killing - direct murder by the mother herself. And we read in the Scripture, for God says very clearly: Even if a mother could forget her child - I will not forget you - I have carved you in the palm of my hand. We are carved in the palm of His hand, so close to Him; that unborn child has been carved in the hand of God. And that is what strikes me most, the beginning of that sentence, that even if a mother could forget something impossible - but even if she could forget - I will not forget you. And today the greatest means - the greatest destroyer of peace is abortion.

And we who are standing here - our parents wanted us. We would not be here if our parents would do that to us. Our children, we want them, we love them, but what of the millions? Many people are very, very concerned with the children in India, with the children in Africa where quite a number die, maybe of malnutrition, of hunger and so on, but millions are dying deliberately by the will of the mother. And this is what is the greatest destroyer of peace today. Because if a mother can kill her own child - what is left for me to kill you and you kill me - there is nothing between. And this I appeal in India, I appeal everywhere: Let us bring the child back, and this year being the child's year: What have we done for the child? At the beginning of the year I told, I spoke everywhere and I said: Let us make this year that we make every single child born, and unborn, wanted. And today is the end of the year, have we really made the children wanted?

I will give you something terrifying. We are fighting abortion by adoption, we have saved thousands of lives, we have sent words to all the clinics, to the hospitals, police stations - please don't destroy the child, we will take the child. So every hour of the day and night it is always somebody, we have quite a number of unwedded mothers - tell them come, we will take care of you, we will take the child from you, and we will get a home for the child. And we have a tremendous demand from families who have no children, that is the blessing of God for us. And also, we are doing another thing which is very beautiful - we are teaching our beggars, our leprosy patients, our slum dwellers, our people of the street, natural family planning.

And in Calcutta alone in six years - it is all in Calcutta -

we have had 61,273 babies less from the families who would have had, but because they practise this natural way of abstaining, of self-control, out of love for each other. We teach them the temperature meter which is very beautiful, very simple, and our poor people understand. And you know what they have told me? Our family is healthy, our family is united, and we can have a baby whenever we want. So clear - those people in the street, those beggars - and I think that if our people can do like that how much more you and all the others who can know the ways and means without destroying the life that God has created in us.

The poor people are very great people. They can teach us so many beautiful things. The other day one of them came to thank and said: You people who have vowed chastity, you are the best people to teach us family planning. Because it is nothing more than self-control out of love for each other. And I think they said a beautiful sentence. And these are people who maybe have nothing to eat, maybe they have not a home where to live, but they are great people. The poor are very wonderful people. One evening we went out and we picked up four people from the street. And one of them was in a most terrible condition - and I told the Sisters: You take care of the other three, I take of this one that looked worse. So I did for her all that my love can do. I put her in bed, and there was such a beautiful smile on her face. She took hold of my hand, as she said one word only: Thank you - and she died.

I could not help but examine my conscience before her, and I asked what would I say if I was in her place. And my answer was very simple. I would have tried to draw a little attention to myself, I would have said I am hungry, that I am dying,

I am cold, I am in pain, or something, but she gave me much more - she gave me her grateful love. And she died with a smile on her face. As that man whom we picked up from the drain, half eaten with worms, and we brought him to the home. 'I have lived like an animal in the street, but I am going to die like an angel, loved and cared for.' And it was so wonderful to see the greatness of that man who could speak like that, who could die like that without blaming anybody, without cursing anybody, without comparing anything. Like an angel - this is the greatness of our people. And that is why we believe what Jesus had said: I was hungry - I was naked - I was homeless - I was unwanted, unloved, uncared for - and you did it to me.

I believe that we are not real social workers. We may be doing social work in the eyes of the people, but we are really contemplatives in the heart of the world. For we are touching the Body of Christ 24 hours. We have 24 hours in this presence, and so do you and I. You too try to bring that presence of God in your family, for the family that prays together stays together. And I think that we in our family don't need bombs and guns, to destroy to bring peace - just get together, love one another, bring that peace, that joy, that strength of presence of each other in the home. And we will be able to overcome all the evil that is in the world.

There is so much suffering, so much hatred, so much misery, and we with our prayer, with our sacrifice are beginning at home. Love begins at home, and it is not how much we do, but how much love we put in the action that we do. It is to God Almighty - how much we do it does not matter, because He is infinite, but how much love we put in that action. How much we do to Him in the person that we are serving.

Some time ago in Calcutta we had great difficulty in getting sugar, and I don't know how the word got around to the children, and a little boy of four years old, a Hindu boy, went home and told his parents: I will not eat sugar for three days. I will give my sugar to Mother Teresa for her children. After three days his father and mother brought him to our home. I had never met them before, and this little one could scarcely pronounce my name, but he knew exactly what he had come to do. He knew that he wanted to share his love.

And this is why I have received such a lot of love from you all. From the time that I have come here I have simply been surrounded with love, and with real, real understanding love. It could feel as if everyone in India, everyone in Africa is somebody very special to you. And I felt quite at home, as I was telling Sister today. I feel in the Convent with the Sisters as if I am in Calcutta with my own Sisters. So completely at home here, right here.

And so here I am talking with you - I want you to find the poor here, right in your own home first. And begin love there. Be that good news to your own people. And find out about your next-door neighbour - do you know who they are? I had the most extraordinary experience with a Hindu family who had eight children. A gentleman came to our house and said: Mother Teresa, there is a family with eight children, they had not eaten for so long - do something. So I took some rice and I went there immediately. And I saw the children - their eyes shining with hunger - I don't know if you have ever seen hunger. But I have seen it very often. And the mother took the rice, she divided the rice, and she went out. When she came back I asked her - where did you go, what did you do? And she gave me a very simple answer: They are hungry also. What struck me most was that she knew - and who are they, a Muslim family - and she knew. I didn't bring more rice that evening because I wanted them to enjoy the joy of sharing. But there were those children, radiating joy, sharing the joy with their mother because she had the love to give. And you see this is where love begins - at home. And I want you - and I am very grateful for what I have received. It has been a tremendous experience and I go back to India - I will be back by next week, the 15th I hope - and I will be able to bring your love.

And I know well that you have not given from your abundance, but you have given until it has hurt you. Today the little children they have - I was so surprised - there is so much joy for the children that are hungry. That the children like themselves will need love and care and tenderness, like they get so much from their parents. So let us thank God that we have had this opportunity to come to know each other, and this knowledge of each other has brought us very close. And we will be able to help not only the children of India and Africa, but will be able to help the children of the whole world, because as you know our Sisters are all over the world. And with this prize that I have received as a prize of peace, I am going to try to make the home for many people that have no home. Because I believe that love begins at home, and if we can create a home for the poor - I think that more and more love will spread. And we will be able through this understanding love to bring peace, be the good news to the poor. The poor in our own family first, in our country and in the world.

To be able to do this, our Sisters, our lives have to be woven with prayer. They have to be woven with Christ to be able to understand, to be able to share. Because today there is so much suffering - and I feel that the passion of Christ is being relived all over again - are we there to share that passion, to share that suffering of people. Around the world, not only in the poor countries, but I found the poverty of the West so much more difficult to remove. When I pick up a person from the street, hungry, I give him a plate of rice, a piece of bread, I have satisfied. I have removed that hunger. But a person that is shut out, that feels unwanted, unloved, terrified, the person that has been thrown out from society - that poverty is so hurting and so much, and I find that very difficult. Our Sisters are working amongst that kind of people in the West. So you must pray for us that we may be able to be that good news, but we cannot do that without you, you have to do that here in your country. You must come to know the poor, maybe our people here have material things, everything, but I think that if we all look into our own homes, how difficult we find it sometimes to smile at each, other, and that the smile is the beginning of love.

And so let us always meet each other with a smile, for the smile is the beginning of love, and once we begin to love each other naturally we want to do something. So you pray for our Sisters and for me and for our Brothers, and for our Co-Workers that are around the world. That we may remain faithful to the gift of God, to love Him and serve Him in the poor together with you. What we have done we should not have been able to do if you did not share with your prayers, with your gifts, this continual giving. But I don't want you to give me from your abundance, I want that you give me until it hurts.

The other day I received 15 dollars from a man who has

been on his back for twenty years, and the only part that he can move is his right hand. And the only companion that he enjoys is smoking. And he said to me: I do not smoke for one week, and I send you this money. It must have been a terrible sacrifice for him, but see how beautiful, how he shared, and with that money I bought bread and I gave to those who were hungry. With a joy on both sides, he was giving and the poor were receiving. This is something that you and I can give - it is a gift of God to us to be able to share our love with others. And let it be as it was for Jesus. Let us love one another as he loved us. Let us love Him with undivided love. And the joy of loving Him and each other - let us give now - that Christmas is coming so close. Let us keep that joy of loving Jesus in our hearts. And share that joy with all that we come in touch with. And that radiating joy is real, for we have no reason not to be happy because we have no Christ with us. Christ in our hearts, Christ in the poor that we meet, Christ in the smile that we give and the smile that we receive. Let us make that one point: That no child will be unwanted, and also that we meet each other always with a smile, especially when it is difficult to smile.

I never forget some time ago about fourteen professors came from the United States from different universities. And they came to Calcutta to our house. Then we were talking about them having been to the home for the dying. We have a home for the dying in Calcutta, where we have picked up more than 36,000 people only from the streets of Calcutta, and out of that big number more than 18,000 have died a beautiful death. They have just gone home to God; and they came to our house and we talked of love, of compassion, and then one of them asked me: Say, Mother, please tell us something that we will remember, and I said to them: Smile at each other, make time for each other in your family. Smile at each other. And then another one asked me: Are you married, and I said: Yes, and I find it sometimes very difficult to smile at Jesus because he can be very demanding sometimes.

This is really something true, and there is where love comes - when it is demanding, and yet we can give it to Him with joy. Just as I have said today, I have said that if I don't go to Heaven for anything else I will be going to Heaven for all the publicity because it has purified me and sacrificed me and made me really ready to go to Heaven. I think that this is something, that we must live life beautifully, we have Jesus with us and He loves us. If we could only remember that God loves me, and I have an opportunity to love others as he loves me, not in big things, but in small things with great love, then Norway becomes a nest of love. And how beautiful it will be that from here a centre for peace has been given. That from here the joy of life of the unborn child comes out. If you become a burning light in the world of peace, then really the Nobel Peace Prize is a gift of the Norwegian people. God bless you!

JRD TATA

1982

Historic Flight Re-enactment

Former chairman of India's most revered company Tata Sons, Jehangir Ratanji Dadabhoy Tata was an accomplished business tycoon and a pioneering aviator. In 1925, J.R.D. joined Tata Sons and was elected chairman in 1938. Under his able chairmanship, the company grew tremendously, from 14 enterprises to a conglomerate of 95 businesses in July, 1988. Meanwhile, he was inspired by Louis Blériot, the popular French aviator, and accompanied by his love for flying, J.R.D. went on to become the first pilot license holder in India. He further came to be known as the Father of Indian Civil Aviation. In 1932, he founded India's first commercial airline, Tata Airlines, later becoming Air India. He has been honoured with the French Legion of Honour and with the Bharat Ratna, India's highest civilian award, in 1992.

On October 15, 1932, J.R.D. undertook his historic 'first flight of the subcontinent' from Karachi to Bombay, for the inaugural Delhi-Bombay flight. Thirty years later in 1962, he re-enacted the same flight from Karachi to Bombay to commemorate Air India's 30th anniversary. This was repeated once again in October 1982 during Indian civil aviation's 50th anniversary, after which J.R.D. delivered this speech to an enthusiastic crowd. The 78 year old flying wizard flew the 50-year old De Havilland Leopard Moth, wanting to instil a spirit of adventure among the younger generation.

In this inspiring speech, J.R.D. humbly wishes for the young generation to have a spirit of adventure in them, to stop the sense of disenchantment he felt was creeping in the country, for fewer people hold hopeful attitudes and the zest for life. With this dedicated flight, he hoped to have 'rekindled a spark of enthusiasm' in the young, for when they grow old, they would also be content with having done all they could, just like he did.

Historic Flight Re-enactment, 1982

It has been said at times that there are moments in life when one feels that if there was a nice big hole in front of one, he would gladly plunge into it. This is one such moment, as I have never been as embarrassed in my life as I have been this evening, listening to speeches about me.

His Excellency the Governor has been good enough to say that I am a modest man. I have usually felt that I have plenty to be modest about. And even today, in flying to Karachi and bringing back a perfectly safe aeroplane- an old lady, it is true, but one who gets on very well with her old pilot- I did not feel that I was doing anything that required great skill, courage or competence. I did not have to cross high mountains, or to battle with snowstorms or fog. On both these occasions, as also fifty years ago, the flight was a relatively simple one of merely staying the air and navigating with reasonable accuracy. There was, it is true, one difference this time. Fifty years ago, the only means I had to navigate was to look at the map and at the ground passing below me, follow a compass and hope that I was going to end up where I intended to. Today, there was a radio to help me. I do feel with no sense of undue modesty that the compliments and congratulations showered on me are greatly in excess of my performance. But I won't say that I didn't enjoy hearing them, however undeserving of them I may feel and I am terribly grateful for them.

Right from childhood, I have been mad about flying and anxiously waited for the day when I would fly myself. I read about every well-known pilot from the beginnings of aviation and was enthralled by their feats. Lindbergh's flight in 1927, in thirty-three hours across the Atlantic in a single-engined plane that was at least six years older than this one, was the kind of achievement that would merit all that has been said today.

I am a little disappointed that I have not been asked, 'Why the hell did you do it, if it was so simple?' In fact, I was asked that in 1962 when I did the same thing. At that time I felt – as I feel even more so today – that the birth of civil aviation and commercial aviation in India, and the growth of air transport over a period of thirty years deserved some kind of celebration. I did not think then that twenty years later, at an age approaching seventy-nine, there would either be an aeroplane for me to fly or that I would be fit to fly. So that was the reason then and so was it today.

I felt that I should do something myself to celebrate and commemorate the occasion (Golden Jubilee) and the only thing I was fit for was to fly an aeroplane.

I had also two other reasons. One was that I wanted to dedicate a gesture to those, at first in handfuls, then in hundreds and finally in thousands, the men and women who, over a period of forty-six years had helped me build up Air-India and Indian air transport. I wanted to express in some way my gratitude and pay tribute to them and I did not know of any other way of dramatizing the event than by the personal gesture of this flight. And so to them and to Air-India who sponsored the flight and got the plane repaired, renewed, refurbished, and made flyable, I express today my very deep gratitude for the enthusiasm, for the toil and the sweat they contributed to our joint endeavour and for sharing with me the joys as well as the heartbreaks of the past fifty years.

The other reason which I think motivated me was to relive a memorable occasion of the past, something one often wants to do – for instance, one's engagement or marriage. Some people do it by marrying more than once. But nowadays with taxes as they are, very few people can afford more than one wife. In any case, my wife might have taken a dismal view of any such thought on my part.

I also had another reason. As I got older, I felt distressed that in recent times there was a growing sense of disenchantment in our land, that the hopes, the aspirations, the enthusiasm, the zest, the joy with which freedom was received in our country some thirty-five years ago, and even before that, the achievements that we participated in, including the creation of Air-India had faded, that there was a loss of morale, a loss of belief in ourselves.

When you talk to young people today, their main worry is to get a job. I don't blame them. It is a real worry. But also, there seems no longer to be a feeling that we can do things as well or better than others or even things that others haven't done. So I thought that, perhaps, this flight would rekindle a spark of enthusiasm, a desire to do something for the country and for its good name, and that it would show that even in these days, when aviation is no longer an adventure but only big business, the times for pioneering are not gone. There are many other things that can be done and many things that the young of this country can do and must steel themselves to doing, however difficult, however discouraging at times the environment, the conditions may be.

And so, in a small way, this flight of mine today was intended to inspire a little hope and enthusiasm in the younger people of our country. I want them to feel, those who are today at a stage of their life I was at in 1932 (fifty years ago), that when they are seventy-eight – and I hope they all will live at least to seventy-eight – they will feel like I do, that despite all the difficulties, all the frustrations, there is a joy in having done something as well as you could and better than others thought you could. I thank you all for your presence.

INDIRA GANDHI

1984

The Last Speech

The fourth Prime Minister of India, Indira Gandhi was a central figure in the Indian National Congress Party. She was the only child of Prime Minister Pandit Jawaharlal Nehru, and is India's first and longest serving female Prime Minister. A leader with a pan-India vision, she made tremendous contribution to the Indian economy. Due to the declaration of the state of emergency in 1975, she was criticized for shutting off the media on June 12, when the emergency was declared, which brought about her downfall in the next elections. The only Prime Minister to be imprisoned after holding office, she fought her next elections from jail and returned to power. Her sheer will and determination led her to be called the 'Iron Lady'.

She was assassinated on October 31, 1984, outside her Delhi residence by two of her bodyguards, following the aftermath of Operation Blue Star. Following her assassination were the appalling Sikh riots, where thousands of Sikhs were killed in Northern India. A day before her assassination, on October 30, 1984, Indira Gandhi visited Orissa and delivered her last public speech at the then Parade Ground in front of the Secretariat of Orissa. Following her death, the Parade Ground was converted to the Indira Gandhi Park.

This speech eerily resonates with her assassination the next day, for it seems that Gandhi, knowingly or unknowingly prophesied her own death ("I am here today; I may not be here tomorrow"). Apart from this sub-conscious association with the idea of death, Gandhi moved the audience by speaking of India's valour and how it should be utilizing the freedom of the country to perform better in the world. She put forth her vision and ideas for improvement in every possible sphere such as education, healthcare, caste system, language and unity of the country. In her stirring speech, she reaches out to Indians, speaking about nationalism, optimism, India's strength as a nation, along with displaying her vision of a developed India.

India, in our long history, has never attacked any country. There have been many invasions against us. People from outside came here and many of them settled here. They proved to be good Indians. Later, they participated with us in the fight for freedom. When India was invaded after we achieved our freedom, all of them expressed their solidarity with the people of India. They stood like a solid wall and faced the challenges. The prime need of the hour is to revive once again the same spirit of solidarity in the hearts and minds of the people. It is not a case of strengthening the hands of Indira Gandhi alone. It means that the hands of millions of people, who live in India, should be strengthened.

The hands of men and women, old and young, scheduled castes and scheduled tribes, people belonging to backward classes indeed, of everybody who is living in India, should be strengthened. They should have the courage and they should have the strength which will take this country along the road of development. All of us should work hard. It is not only a question of manual labour, it also concerns the mind. Let new ideas be brought in from different sources, so that in this scientific age India could progress.

Whenever I happen to meet scientists I have only one message for them, "Do something which is of use to the whole of the country." But if along with this a scientific temper is not cultivated, if we remain prisoners of superstitions, if we continue to quarrel among ourselves, if we tolerate communalism and do not fight against it, if we let casteism or regionalism develop and grow or if we start quarrelling in the name of language, how will we be able to preserve the unity of India? If unity is not preserved, how will we protect our independence? Do not think that if we have won freedom once, we will be able to preserve it for all time to come. Eternal vigilance is the price of freedom. We have to think about it and do something about it every day. We have to preserve that freedom for our poorer masses, particularly for the people who are backward and are living in backward areas. We should make freedom a reality for them.

Actually, the real work started from that point and the Congress took upon itself two things. First, democracy should be nurtured because until each and everybody's voice is not heard, freedom would not be complete. Secondly, the congress adopted the path of socialism. Without economic equality, and without equal opportunities for all, freedom could not be considered complete. If there are acute inequalities in the society, the gap between the rich and the poor will widen, resulting in increased tension and class struggle.

If there is no peace in the society, freedom cannot be secure and development projects cannot be executed, progress cannot be made. Therefore, from the very beginning we made strides towards self-reliance. If you travel, you will see how the picture of our country is changing in post-independence India. As we go forward, we face new problems. There are chronic problems, like poverty and economic backwardness. But there are also problems which are the result of progress and development.

Several countries are rich. Even then, they have failed to root out unemployment, or control rising prices. As a matter of fact, both the problems have aggravated there in the recent years. Even then, we have to find out a way, so that we are able to avoid these problems. These are not new challenges. These are old problems and we are making efforts to solve them. How will unemployment be removed, and how do we get over price rise? When we increase our production, the people will get employment opportunities. We have also to see that when production is increased and we achieve success, the fruits of these reach all the people.

We have to take to the masses our programs regarding education and health care, particularly to those areas where people have been victims of social and economic injustice for centuries. This must be remedied. This is our object and we are moving towards that direction. We were doing it before, we are doing it now and we will continue to pursue our path as before whether we are in office or out of office.

So, everything is interrelated. We have to co-ordinate everything and move forward. We have to strike a balance in our social structure. We can do this only when there is peace in the society. If agitations coupled with violence are launched and people hate each other and the opposition parties encourage such agitations without considering the long-term effects on the social fabric of our country, then we will not be successful. All of us must think how much pain, agony and hardship it will cause to our countrymen.

Some agitations have been launched which have harmed the country's unity. The slogans which are raised by these agitators were not originated in this country. These have been coined in foreign countries by those who live outside India. Many anti-social and treacherous elements found their way into these agitations. In the shadow of these agitations, they indulge in evil work. What happened in Punjab is known to all of you.

What was happening in Jammu and Kashmir is also known to you. It was not a question of an individual at any place. Neither was it a question of a particular caste or creed or religion or party. The real question was that the things which were happening were not beneficial to the country and were creating difficulties for India. They were likely to create hazards and crises in the country in future. But no government can support any deed or any action which would weaken the country, whatever the price.

The citizens of India must think of India first. We may belong to any religion or caste or creed, but nationalism is supreme, the love for our country must get priority over everything. But today some people think that they should support or back any agitation which may help in getting votes to them during the elections. But the people in Orissa and the people living in different states and indeed the people of the whole country, must realize that such agitations will pose a greater danger to our country.

Our policy is to have friendly relations with all countries. But we shall not give up our self-respect or overlook the interest of India. Many times India has faced invasions and there were five attacks in recent years. We should always be prepared to face such a contingency. We have already assured our people and the people of the world that we will never attack anybody. We shall continue to pursue our policy of friendship with all people. The same is our policy at home.

Our progress has been acknowledged by other nations. Be it big universities or big international economic organizations, everybody acknowledges that India has pursued the path of progress, despite difficulties, without incurring big debts or without being trapped into any crisis. Since 1980, every year, we have done something or the other which is remarkable and every time it has helped to enhance the reputation of the country in the comity of nations. The young generation of India and the intellectuals of this country have new opportunities to achieve name and fame and expand their scope of knowledge. That is why we have to see that India continues to move forward on this path.

India does not raise her voice only for her own sake. If we raise our voice it is not on behalf of the Congress. We are speaking here on behalf of the people of India, on behalf of the weaker sections of India, on behalf of the women of India, on behalf of the intellectuals of India and above all, on behalf of the younger generation of India, for the future belongs to them. If they move forward on the right path and if they engage themselves in constructive activities and do not indulge in sabotage then a bright future awaits them.

They can also build their states and the country. So this is our view for India. This applies to all the under-developed nations of the world. What we say here is also criticized. Our aid is discontinued. But wherever injustice is perpetrated, India always is the first to raise its voice against it because we know if there is injustice at one place and the people are suppressed, then it will affect the whole world.

My father used to say that freedom cannot be divided. In the same manner, progress is also indivisible, development is also indivisible. Many countries of the world have become prosperous through scientific development and they are also collecting wealth very rapidly and using it for raising their standard. They are very powerful and even then, they want to influence other nations.

It is not like the older type of slavery. In that system, imperialist powers used to dispatch their forces and occupy territory. But in the new system, they try to influence people by their ideology. They try to break the morale of the people. Even if the weaker nations do some good work, the powers try to show that the under-developed countries have done nothing.

I had to resort to emergency for a very brief period. But even today I am being criticized. I am being described as authoritarian and dictatorial. But the same people are fully helping the other authoritarian regimes with money, resources and arms. For them that dictatorship is not dictatorship. Therefore, we have to learn from all this and know after all what they want, why they want India should not go forward. No outsider will take care of our interest or think about us. We have to look after ourselves. This is not exclusively my responsibility.

I am here today; I may not be here tomorrow. But the

responsibility to look after national interest is on the shoulder of every citizen of India. I have often mentioned this earlier. Nobody knows how many attempts have been made to shoot me; lathis have been used to beat me. In Bhubaneswar itself, a brickbat hit me. They have attacked me in every possible manner. I do not care whether I live or die. I have lived a long life and I am proud that I spend the whole of my life in the service of my people. I am only proud of this and nothing else. I shall continue to serve until my last breath and when I die, I can say that every drop of my blood will invigorate India and strengthen it.

I hope that youth, women and others, all will think together. They should shoulder the responsibilities and it cannot be done by accepting others as leaders. Leaders come and go.

When the struggle for freedom was on, many times we were in jail. But because of our absence, the struggle never ceased. In every state, province and district, new leaders came up. It is our wish that every section of the people living in Orissa, whether they are from scheduled tribes or happen to belong to any other caste, will think, "This is my country. This is our country". We must make our nation strong. We must reinforce its integration and it is our responsibility, it is every citizen's responsibility. We cannot make Indira Gandhi or the Congress or any other leader responsible for this work. We want that this spirit should develop and envelop the country.

When we talk about self-reliance, it means we want self-reliance in the material sense. But we also want psychological self-reliance. The people must feel confident that they have the strength to do the job and I know that this strength is the in the masses. I fully believe that the masses of India will never take a wrong path. The people of the world know about it. Many cultures and civilizations have disappeared into oblivion. But as the poet Iqbal once said, 'We have survived, whereas all those ancient civilizations have perished. Our civilization is still there.'

It means that there is some inherent strength in us; that is why we are surviving. That strength is there inside everybody. But you have to let it develop. If you do not allow it to develop, if you are frustrated, then the inner strength will not take its shape and it will work negatively. There are weaknesses and we have to fight those weaknesses. But if we do not have the courage, if we do not have the necessary morale, then we shall not be able to get over those shortcomings and weaknesses. Without doing this, good work cannot be done. So, it is in your hands, in the hands of the people of Orissa and in the hand of the people of this country what they want to do.

We can only formulate policies and programs. We are there to help. But development work must go on. You must see that Orissa progresses. It is your responsibility. Everybody should search his heart and ask himself why he would do this job. I fully believe that this beautiful state, where art and other things have developed so much, will also develop economically. You should not do anything to strike at the roots of your art or traditions. These should also develop along with economic progress.

You have heard me very patiently. I shall repeat that you must give top priority to the unity and integrity of the country. Everything else is secondary. We have to face today's challenges in such a manner that we emerge stronger and our strength continues to grow. If we gain something for the short term and if it weakens us tomorrow or day after, then it is not a thing worth pursuing.

Jai Hind.

ATAL BIHARI VAJPAYEE

2001

United Nations General Assembly Speech

Atal Bihari Vajpayee is one of the most respected Prime Ministers of India, serving his Prime Ministerial tenure from 1998 to 2004. A great statesman, Mr Vajpayee is accepted as the greatest of modern times. His first brush with nationalist politics was in 1942 when he joined the Quit India Movement during his student days. Having a keen interest in foreign affairs, Vajpayee kept his knowledge updated, which was then put to good use when he later represented India in various international forays. For a short while, he acted as a journalist and edited Rashtradharma (a Hindi monthly), Panchjanya (a Hindi weekly) and dailies Swades and Veer Arjun, before joining the Bhartiya Jana Sangh in 1951. He is also a talented poet with several publications. Known for the love for Hindi language, he is the first person to deliver a speech in the United Nations General Assembly in 1977.

Under his tenure as Prime Minister, India conducted underground nuclear tests in 1998 in Pokhran, which were considered a national milestone. Vajpayee also introduced many economic and infrastructural reforms such as strengthening of private sectors, encouraging private research and development and privatizing Government owned enterprises. The

Sarva Shiksha Abhiyaan, aimed at provision of elementary education for all, was also started by him. His perception as a capable and wise leader was further strengthened with his effective handling of serious issues such as the Kargil War of 1999. As a gesture of harmony and breaking physical as well as mental barriers, he travelled to Lahore in the Delhi-Lahore bus on February 20, 1999.

The following speech was delivered at the 56th session of the United Nations General Assembly in 2001 on November 10, 2001, shortly after the historic 9/11 attacks in New York City and Washington DC. Vajpayee reflected on the terrorist attack, speaking of unity and rejecting any propagation of empathy due to the so-called 'root causes' of terrorist activity. He also talked about the state of poverty and role of globalization in constricting development and suggested possible solutions to reduce global poverty.

Mr. President, I congratulate you on your election as President of the 56th General Assembly. I also take this opportunity to warmly congratulate the Secretary General, Mr. Kofi Annan, and the United Nations on being honoured with the Nobel Peace Prize.

This session of the General Assembly is being held in the shadow of the barbaric terrorist acts of September 11, which dramatically reminded us that neither distance nor power insulates a State from terrorism. They represented an arrogant rejection of the values of freedom and tolerance, which democratic and pluralistic societies cherish. Even while uniting the nations of the world in their grief, this terrible tragedy has created the opportunity to fashion a determined global response to terrorism in all its forms and manifestations, wherever it exists and under whatever name. We in India know from our own bitter experience that terrorists develop global networks driven by religious extremism. Their operations are supported by drug trafficking, money laundering and arms smuggling. Some States follow a policy of sponsoring and sheltering them. They can only be countered through closely coordinated efforts of the international community.

The UN Security Council resolutions 1368 and 1373 are steps in the right direction, but it requires firm political will of the freedom-loving world to implement them rigorously. The two crucial elements in this would be strict curbs on sources of financing for terrorists and denying them safe havens for training, arming and operation.

We must firmly rebuff any ideological, political or religious justification for terrorism. We should reject self-serving arguments seeking to classify terrorism according to its root causes, and therefore justifying terrorist action somewhere while condemning it elsewhere. Those that advance these arguments should explain what the root causes of the brutal acts of September 11 were.

Mr. President, India supports the current campaign against the terrorist networks in Afghanistan. We hope that it reaches an early and successful conclusion. That country's current travails can only end with the establishment of a broad-based, representative and neutral government, which would stop the export of terrorism and extremism. The international community should work towards this even while the military campaign continues, so that we avoid a political vacuum at the end of the campaign.

We must recognize that current structures to facilitate a post-Taleban political settlement are unrepresentative and therefore ineffective. Located as it is in Afghanistan's neighbourhood, India's vital national interests are affected by developments in it. We also have traditionally close links with Afghanistan. This is the basis for our belief that India can play a useful role in this process.

The task of reconstruction in post-conflict Afghanistan also merits the urgent attention of the international community. It would require massive external assistance to create an economic situation conducive to the speedy return and rehabilitation of the millions of Afghans who have taken refuge in other countries of this region. Again India stands ready to join international efforts for this. We have already announced relief assistance of a million tonnes of wheat, medicines and medical assistance for needy Afghans within and outside the country. We have also pledged 100 million dollars to post-conflict Afghanistan for reconstruction. We are prepared to do more.

Mr. President, nearly six thousand lives were lost on September 11. But the global economic downturn in its aftermath will take a far larger human toll, mainly in the developing world. The World Bank has estimated that tens of thousands more children will die worldwide and some ten million more people are likely to go below the poverty line of 1 dollar a day. It is pertinent to reflect on these chilling statistics even as the Ministerial Conference gets under way in Doha to consider WTO issues.

Before we embark on any new initiatives for globalization and sustainable development, we should recognize that political support for them would be determined primarily by the impact of these regimes on poverty. For most developing countries, the Uruguay Round has done little for economic growth, while poverty levels and income gaps have worsened. Globalization has constrained developing countries in mobilizing public resources for poverty alleviation.

This is why public support for the globalization regime has vanished in developing countries. This is also why we have argued strongly that implementation issues should first be resolved before we try to widen the WTO agenda further. Our public is unwilling to accept another post-dated cheque, when an earlier one has bounced.

Similarly, the movement towards sustainable development has proved a disappointment. Developing countries are unable to realize fair payments for their sovereign biodiversity resources, and traditional knowledge. The treaties on climate change and biodiversity have also failed to activate the anticipated investment and technology transfers to developing countries. Industrialized countries have not shown the political will to enhance their overseas development budgets. Multilateral development agencies are also constrained in their resources, of which, in any case, very little is available on concessional terms.

The inevitable conclusion is that for current regimes of globalization and sustainable development to be strengthened - or even to survive - they must re-engineered to generate large-scale finances for poverty alleviation. The passion for globalization has to be tempered by compassion for its victims. Sadly, this thought has not penetrated into the thinking of the developed economies. Their actions also do not reflect the realization that there cannot be a sustainable revival of their own sluggish economies unless the globalization and sustainable development priorities are re-oriented and anchored in the developmental needs of two-thirds of the global population.

Mr President, a year ago, I had suggested, in my speech to the US Congress, a Comprehensive Global Dialogue on Development. The aim of such a dialogue would be to address the highly unstable situation in which one-third of the world's population lives in luxury and condemns the remaining two-thirds to poverty and want. It is a fertile breeding ground for political unrest, economic chaos, and social fractures.

India would be happy to coordinate this dialogue, with the immediate objective of mobilizing resources for poverty alleviation programmes in developing countries. A preliminary agenda for the dialogue could include:

- The accelerated liquidation of external debts of low income and highly indebted countries;
- Poverty alleviation programmes specifically aimed at developing countries facing financial crises;
- Stabilization of international prices of primary commodity exports; And, most importantly,
- Welfare and development programmes for all the world's needy children, for their nutrition, health, education, and protection from degrading and hazardous employment.

The struggle for equitable development and the war against poverty are as important as our campaign against terrorism and our collective search for security. At a time when an external stimulus has motivated us to unite against terrorism and for security, let us summon an equally strong inner resolve for development and poverty alleviation. They are just as crucial for a global order at peace with itself.

Mr President, this fundamental and seamless linkage between peace, security and development can be recalled in the sage words of the great Indian poet Rabindranath Tagore:

"From now onward, any nation that takes an isolated view of its own interests will run contrary to the spirit of the New Age, and will know no peace. From now onward, the anxiety that each country has for its own safety must embrace the welfare of the whole world."

Thank you.

NARAYANA MURTHY

2007

Pre-commencement Address at New York University

N.R. Narayana Murthy, co-founder of Infosys Technologies Limited, a global software consulting company, is presently the non-executive chairman of the Board and Chief Mentor. He has been listed among the 12 greatest entrepreneurs of our time by Fortune magazine, and described as the 'Father of Indian IT sector' by Time magazine for his contribution to outsourcing in India. He is also a recipient of the Padhma Vibhushan and Padma Shri awards, among other distinguished honours.

An inspiration to all Indians, Narayana Murthy worked his way up to the top rung of the ladder with sheer perseverance, focus on values, and a clear sense of understanding. Now the 33rd richest man in India, he is a role model for budding entrepreneurs in the country.

At this stirring pre-commencement address at New York University (Stern School of Business) on May 9, 2007, Narayana Murthy talked about the lessons he learned from his life and career, and how those helped him grow. The most striking feature of this speech, that was perhaps appreciated wide and far, is the honest tone in his words, that only goes on to strengthen his message and inspire people with a tale of determination and passion. Speaking on the importance of role models in shaping one's life, and about chance events paving way for the better, Narayan Murthy emphasised how being in a crisis situation, or encountering failures rather helped him learn and grow than making him go backward.

It is quite remarkable to know how this entrepreneur swears by age-old values, believes in himself, performs with conviction and takes bold steps wherever necessary. With a perspective of a true leader, Narayana Murthy has been immensely successful in making Infosys among the top companies in the world, contributing significantly to national as well as global growth.

Pre-commencement Address at New York University, 2007

Dean Cooley, faculty, staff, distinguished guests, and, most importantly, the graduating class of 2007

It is a great privilege to speak at your commencement ceremonies. I thank Dean Cooley and Professor Marti Subrahmanyam for their kind invitation. I am exhilarated to be part of such a joyous occasion. Congratulations to you, the class of 2007, on completing an important milestone in your life journey. After some thought, I have decided to share with you some of my life lessons. I learned these lessons in the context of my early career struggles, a life lived under the influence of sometimes unplanned events which were the crucibles that tempered my character and reshaped my future. I would like first to share some of these key life events with you, in the hope that these may help you understand my struggles and how chance events and unplanned encounters with influential persons shaped my life and career. Later, I will share the deeper life lessons that I have learned. My sincere hope is that this sharing will help you see your own trials and tribulations for the hidden blessings they can be.

The first event occurred when I was a graduate student in Control Theory at IIT, Kanpur, in India. At breakfast on a bright Sunday morning in 1968, I had a chance encounter with a famous computer scientist on sabbatical from a well-known US university. He was discussing exciting new developments in the field of computer science with a large group of students and how such developments would alter our future. He was articulate, passionate and quite convincing. I was hooked. I went straight from breakfast to the library, read four or five papers he had suggested, and left the library determined to study computer science. Friends, when I look back today at that pivotal meeting, I marvel at how one role model can alter for the better the future of a young student. This experience taught me that valuable advice can sometimes come from an unexpected source, and chance events can sometimes open new doors.

The next event that left an indelible mark on me occurred in 1974. The location: Nis, a border town between former Yugoslavia, now Serbia, and Bulgaria. I was hitchhiking from Paris back to Mysore, India, my home town. By the time a kind driver dropped me at Nis railway station at 9 p.m. on a Saturday night, the restaurant was closed. So was the bank the next morning, and I could not eat because I had no local money. I slept on the railway platform until 8:30 p.m. in the night when the Sofia Express pulled in. The only passengers in my compartment were a girl and a boy. I struck a conversation in French with the young girl. She talked about the travails of living in an iron curtain country, until we were roughly interrupted by some policemen who, I later gathered, were summoned by the young man who thought we were criticising the communist government of Bulgaria.

The girl was led away; my backpack and sleeping bag were confiscated. I was dragged along the platform into a small 8x8 foot room with a cold stone floor and a hole in one corner by way of toilet facilities. I was held in that bitterly cold room without food or water for over seventy-two hours. I had lost all hope of ever seeing the outside world again, when the door opened. I was again dragged out unceremoniously, locked up in the guard's compartment on a departing freight train and told that I would be released 20 hours later upon reaching Istanbul. The guard's final words still ring in my ears: "You are from a friendly country called India and that is why we are letting you go!" The journey to Istanbul was lonely, and I was starving. This long, lonely, cold journey forced me to deeply rethink my convictions about communism. Early on a dark Thursday morning, after being hungry for one hundred and eight hours, I was purged of any last vestiges of affinity for the Left. I concluded that entrepreneurship, resulting in large-scale job creation, was the only viable mechanism for eradicating poverty in societies. Deep in my heart, I always thank the Bulgarian guards for transforming me from a confused leftist into a determined, compassionate capitalist! Inevitably, this sequence of events led to the eventual founding of Infosys in 1981.

While these first two events were rather fortuitous, the next two, both concerning the Infosys journey, were more planned and profoundly influenced my career trajectory.

On a chilly Saturday morning in the winter of 1990, five of the seven founders of Infosys met in our small office in a leafy Bangalore suburb. The decision at hand was the possible sale of Infosys for the enticing sum of $1 million. After nine years of toil in the then business-unfriendly India, we were quite happy at the prospect of seeing at least some money. I let my younger colleagues talk about their future plans. Discussions about the travails of our journey thus far and our future challenges went on for about four hours. I had not yet spoken a word.

Finally, it was my turn. I spoke about our journey from a small Mumbai apartment in 1981 that had been beset with many challenges, but also of how I believed we were at the darkest hour before the dawn. I then took an audacious step. If they were all bent upon selling the company, I said, I would buy out all my colleagues, though I did not have a cent in my pocket. There was a stunned silence in the room. My colleagues wondered aloud about my foolhardiness. But I remained silent. However, after an hour of my arguments, my colleagues changed their minds to my way of thinking. I urged them that if we wanted to create a great company, we should be optimistic and confident. They have more than lived up to their promise of that day.

In the seventeen years since that day, Infosys has grown to revenues in excess of $3.0 billion, a net income of more than $800 million and a market capitalisation of more than $28 billion, 28,000 times richer than the offer of $1 million on that day. In the process, Infosys has created more than 70,000 well-paying jobs, 2,000-plus dollar-millionaires and 20,000-plus rupee millionaires.

A final story: On a hot summer morning in 1995, a Fortune-10 corporation had sequestered all their Indian software vendors, including Infosys, in different rooms at the Taj Residency hotel in Bangalore so that the vendors could not communicate with one another. This customer's propensity for tough negotiations was well-known. Our team was very nervous. First of all, with revenues of only around $5 million, we were minnows compared to the customer. Second, this customer contributed fully 25% of our revenues. The loss of this business would potentially devastate our recently-listed company. Third, the customer's negotiation style was very aggressive. The customer team would go from room to room, get the best terms out of each vendor and then pit one vendor against the other. This went on for several rounds. Our various arguments why a fair price - one that allowed us to invest in good people, research and development, infrastructure, technology and training - was actually in their interest failed to cut any ice with the customer. By 5 p.m. on the last day, we had to make a decision right on the spot whether to accept the customer's terms or to walk out. All eyes were on me as I mulled over the decision. I closed my eyes, and reflected upon our journey until then. Through many a tough call, we had always thought about the long-term interests of Infosys. I communicated clearly to the customer team that we could not accept their terms, since it could well lead us to letting them down later. But I promised a smooth, professional transition to a vendor of customer's choice. This was a turning point for Infosys.

Subsequently, we created a Risk Mitigation Council which ensured that we would never again depend too much on any one client, technology, country, application area or key employee. The crisis was a blessing in disguise. Today, Infosys has a sound de-risking strategy that has stabilised its revenues and profits. I want to share with you, next, the life lessons these events have taught me.

#1: I will begin with the importance of learning from experience. It is less important, I believe, where you start. It is more important how and what you learn. If the quality of the learning is high, the development gradient is steep, and, given time, you can find yourself in a previously unattainable place. I believe the Infosys story is living proof of this. Learning from experience, however, can be complicated. It can be much more difficult to learn from success than from failure. If we fail, we think carefully about the precise cause. Success can indiscriminately reinforce all our prior actions.

#2: A second theme concerns the power of chance events. As I think across a wide variety of settings in my life, I am struck by the incredible role played by the interplay of chance events with intentional choices. While the turning points themselves are indeed often fortuitous, how we respond to them is anything but so. It is this very quality of how we respond systematically to chance events that is crucial.

#3: Of course, the mindset one works with is also quite critical. As recent work by the psychologist, Carol Dweck, has shown, it matters greatly whether one believes in ability as inherent or that it can be developed. Put simply, the former view, a fixed mindset, creates a tendency to avoid challenges, to ignore useful negative feedback and leads such people to plateau early and not achieve their full potential. The latter view, a growth mindset, leads to a tendency to embrace challenges, to learn from criticism and such people reach ever higher levels of achievement.

#4: The fourth theme is a cornerstone of the Indian spiritual tradition: self-knowledge. Indeed, the highest form of knowledge, it is said, is self-knowledge. I believe this greater awareness and knowledge of oneself is what ultimately helps develop a more grounded belief in oneself, courage, determination, and above all, humility, all qualities which enable one to wear one's success with dignity and grace.

Based on my life experiences, I can assert that it is this belief in learning from experience, a growth mindset, the power of chance events, and self-reflection that have helped me grow to the present. Back in the 1960s, the odds of my being in front of you today would have been zero. Yet here I stand before you! With every successive step, the odds kept changing in my favour, and it is these life lessons that made all the difference.

My young friends, I would like to end with some words of advice.

Do you believe that your future is pre-ordained, and is already set?

Or, do you believe that your future is yet to be written and that it will depend upon the sometimes fortuitous events?

Do you believe that these events can provide turning points to which you will respond with your energy and enthusiasm?

Do you believe that you will learn from these events and that you will reflect on your setbacks?

Do you believe that you will examine your successes with even greater care?

I hope you believe that the future will be shaped by several turning points with great learning opportunities. In fact, this is the path I have walked to much advantage.

A final word: When, one day, you have made your mark on the world, remember that in the ultimate analysis, we are all mere temporary custodians of the wealth we generate, whether it be financial, intellectual, or emotional. The best use of all your wealth is to share it with those less fortunate.

I believe that we have all at some time eaten the fruit from trees that we did not plant. In the fullness of time, when it is our turn to give, it behoves us in turn to plant gardens that we may never eat the fruit of, which will largely benefit generations to come. I believe this is our sacred responsibility, one that I hope you will shoulder in time. Thank you for your patience. Go forth and embrace your future with open arms, and pursue enthusiastically your own life journey of discovery!

VISWANATHAN ANAND

2007

Speech at NIIT, Chennai

Indian chess champion Viswanathan Anand, garnered worldwide acclaim as he bagged the World Chess Champion title five times (in 2000, 2007, 2008, 2010 and 2012). He became India's first 'grandmaster' in the year 1988, by winning the Shakti Finance International chess tournament held in Coimbatore, India. 'Grandmaster' is the highest title a chess player can attain worldwide. He has received many other notable awards such as the Rajiv Gandhi Khel Ratna Award (1991-1992), Chess Oscars (1997, 1998, 2003, 2004, 2007 and 2008) and the Padma Shri (1987). He is also the first sportsperson in Indian history to receive the Padhma Vibhushan, the second highest civilian award in India.

Having been exposed to the game at the outset, at the age of six, Anand was taken to the game in Chennai, home to chess champions Manuel Aaron and Ravi Kumar. Starting off his career at a very early age, Viswanathan Anand was the youngest Asian to win the International Master's Title at the age of fifteen and became the National Chess Champion at the age of sixteen. He has been playing games at blitz speed, that is, a fast pace, and playing in big events never slowed him down. He is credited with lifting Indian chess to new heights, with his tremendous success at national and international levels.

In June 2007, Viswanathan Anand addressed the students of NIIT in Chennai and delivered this stimulating speech. Anand in his speech highlighted the relevance of goal clarity as the most important ingredient to success. He spoke of his own experience and his journey as a chess player since an early age. He provides suggestions for improvement, applicable to everyone in any field. This simple, yet awe-inspiring speech by an admirably exceptional player manages to give a rare perspective into the game and is truly a jewel in terms of inspiration.

Speech at NIIT, Chennai, 2007

I started playing chess at the age of six. I used to observe my elder siblings play chess and asked my mom if I could learn the game too. I never really thought I would make it big. I just enjoyed playing chess. My sister decided I should join a chess club. Three days after joining the club I realised I could play my first tournament. I don't know if it was such a bright idea but when you are six, optimism is never a problem.

I promptly lost my first three games in the tournament; the fourth I won by default. My opponent failed to turn up. I counted the seconds, anxiously praying that my rival wouldn't turn up at the last minute and spoil the fun. This was my first victory in chess. From then on, I played in many weekend events and state-level tournaments. There was no specific goal or big picture. It was just a natural progression from one level to the other.

The Holy Grail of Indian chess till 1987 was when and who would become India's first Grandmaster. I chased the Grandmaster title for two whole years. Every time I would come close enough, but would miss it by the narrowest margin. At the end of 1986 I took a small break from chess and decided to do something unusual. I prepared for my exams. I was so happy to study for my Class 12 exams. My fellow students found it difficult to grasp that preparing for exams could be pleasurable. Right after my Class 12 exam, I won the World

Junior and subsequently the Grandmaster title.

Sometimes when you have a goal in front of you it is easy to focus. Cyclists have pelotons who give them that focus as to what they should achieve in short bursts. After becoming a Grandmaster I realised I no longer had a goal. It didn't matter whether I scored 5 or 6 points in a tournament. Soon, my results started to decline. As long as you know what your destination is, you know how fast you want to get there. But once you have reached your destination you start looking back rather looking at new peaks.

When I played the Linares tournament in 1991, I beat Anatoly Karpov. I was offered a bonus if I defeated Karpov. I thought if I do beat him I would pay the organiser my bonus. When I first defeated Karpov I realised I could play the Soviet Grandmasters and even defeat them. Slowly guys started trash-talking me. People used to describe me as a talent, so this was a new experience. Later I realised that when they flatter you it means they show pity. And when they actually say something negative, it means they respect you.

I slowly started to understand that the occasional win over Karpov or Garry Kasparov wasn't enough. One had to play the whole event well and be consistent. In the beginning, beating anyone among the top five Grandmasters in an event would more or less make me content. After going through four or five events with just an upset over a top seed, I thought of actually trying to be a top player. I had to make a podium finish and even aim for first place.

This happened in Regio Emilia when I beat both Karpov

and Kasparov and won the event. I think I used all these lessons came together in 2000 when I became the World Champion. Soon after winning the most exalted title a sportsperson can aspire to, came the vacuum. What was the next big thing?

I did have some good results, but crisis struck in the Dortmund tournament in 2001. I started with two losses and tried hard not to lose. Then I lost a further game. Thinking I had hit rock bottom, I decided to play very passively. I was duly punished with a fourth defeat. This was my worst performance ever. So what went wrong in Dortmund?

I had done some good preparation. I was very disciplined and kept up my routine. But the spark was missing. I was so scared of avoiding failure and taking risks that I was staring the abyss in the face. It is extremely difficult to change a winning formula, but one has to experiment even when you succeed. Defeat gives you the courage to experiment. Success can never motivate you the same way.

After Dortmund I decided I had to do something different. I decided to work on new areas. I went through several months of indifferent results. After a few months I played a rapid Grand Prix in Dubai. I was eliminated in the second round. This was quite a rude shock as rapid chess was always my forte. The tournament had a strange rule that meant that even if you were eliminated you played on for the final standings. So I thought I could have seven days of suffering and silent torture or have one week of fun and play chess. I decided to take the second route. I played different openings, stopped worrying about results. All of a sudden, I was Anand, the six-year-old boy. The same boy who played chess at lightning speed, the one who could calculate fast and who thoroughly enjoyed the game.

AR RAHMAN

2009

Oscar Awards Acceptance

Allah-Rakha Rahman is a well-known and accomplished Indian composer, singer-songwriter, music producer, musician and philanthropist. Regarded as the 'Mozart of Madras' for his unique contribution to film and music, Rahman has composed songs that amalgamate elements of different music systems and genres, such as carnatic, western classical, Hindustani and the qawwali style of Nusrat Fateh Ali Khan. He has written songs for more than 130 films since 1992 and has been the recipient of many awards and honours in the film and music industry, including two Academy Awards (Oscars), two Grammy Awards, a BAFTA Award, A Golden Globe, fifteen Filmfare Awards, among others. Time magazine hailed him as 'the world's most prominent and prolific film composer' in 2009.

Rahman is popularly known as the man who redefined contemporary Indian music. His popular soundtracks and albums include his first soundtrack for Roja, also hailed by Time among the '10 Best Soundtracks' in 2005, Dil Se, Taal, Lagaan, Vandemataram, Jodhaa Akbar, Slumdog Millionaire and Rockstar. He is a big believer in music and film, and feels that music has the power to bring people together, with love.

On February 22, 2009, A.R. Rahman bagged two Oscars for his contribution to the film Slumdog Millionaire. While Rahman, along with fellow composer Gulzar, won the 'Best Song' Oscar for the soul-uplifting song Jai Ho, he also accepted the Oscar for 'Best Original Score'. In this acceptance speech, Rahman gives due credit to his mother Kareema Begum, who had made a trip from Chennai to witness this proud moment at the Kodak Theatre. His short, yet joyous speech won hearts and reflected the man's passion, gratitude and simplicity. While he was receiving this honour, his family back in Chennai was cutting a cake and rejoicing in this achievement. Winning Oscars has been a national pride and this was an occasion to celebrate. Tamil Nadu Chief Minister had commented, "Isai (Music) in Tamil means Puhazh (fame). True to this, today, Rahman, born in Chennai, has blossomed and reached the pinnacle and earned a place in the hearts of the entire artist community in the world. It is a great honour for our son".

Oscar Awards Acceptance, 2009

Before coming, I was excited and terrified. The last time I felt like that was during my marriage. There's a dialogue from a Hindi film, "Mere paas ma hai," which means, "I have nothing but I have a mother." So mother's here, her blessings are there with me. I am grateful for her to have come all the way. And I want to thank the Academy for being so kind, all the jury members. I want to thank Sam Schwartz, I/D PR, all the crew of 'Slumdog,' Mr. Gulzar, Raqueeb Alam, Blaaze, my musicians in Chennai and Mumbai. And I want to say something in Tamil, which I normally say after every award. It is: Ella puhazhum iraivanukke. "God is great." Thank you.

APJ ABDUL KALAM

2011

Vision for India

Former President of India, Dr. APJ Abdul Kalam is among the most revered leaders in the country. A scientist and aerospace engineer by profession, he is popularly known as the 'Missile Man of India', appreciated for his work on development of the ballistic missile and launch vehicle technology. He has also been the recipient of many honours and awards, including the Bharat Ratna in 1997, for his immense contribution to the scientific research and modernization of defence technology in India. Dr. Kalam has authored inspiring books including Ignited Minds, Wings of Fire and India 2020. He is also known as 'People's President' due to his unconventional working style and is quite fond of children.

Known for his motivational and inspiring speeches to the youth of the country, Dr. Kalam is a frequent addresser. In this speech delivered at Indian Institute of Technology, Hyderabad, Kalam put forth his vision for India, clearly stating his belief in the strength of our country. He lays out three ideas as visions for the country: freedom, development and the strength to stand up to the world.

He addresses the youth, for he feels the young have the

ability to bring about the much-needed change that can make India stand at par with any other developed nation. Dr. Kalam stresses on the power of individuals to make things better, by advocating the importance of having the right kind of attitude. Using inspiring examples taken from his experiences, Dr. Kalam gives a glimpse of how wonderful India can be. Abdul Kalam truly is a man with vision, and holds a passion to spread this enthusiasm for the country to the youth, as is evident from his addresses to the student population.

I have three visions for India. In 3000 years of our history, people from all over the world have come and invaded us, captured our lands, conquered our minds. From Alexander onwards, The Greeks, the Turks, the Moguls, the Portuguese, the British, the French, the Dutch, all of them came and looted us, took over what was ours. Yet we have not done this to any other nation. We have not conquered anyone. We have not grabbed their land, their culture, their history and tried to enforce our way of life on them. Why? Because we respect the freedom of others.

That is why my first vision is that of freedom. I believe that India got its first vision of this in 1857, when we started the war of Independence. It is this freedom that we must protect and nurture and build on. If we are not free, no one will respect us.

My second vision for India is its development. For fifty years we have been a developing nation. It is time we see ourselves as a developed nation. We are among the top five nations of the world in terms of GDP. We have 10 percent growth rate in most areas. Our poverty levels are falling. Our achievements are being globally recognized today. Yet, we lack the self-confidence to see ourselves as a developed nation, self-reliant and self-assured. Isn't this incorrect?

I have a third vision. India must stand up to the world. I believe that unless India stands up to the world, no one will respect us. Only strength respects strength. We must be strong, not only as a military power but also as an economic power. Both must go hand-in-hand.

My good fortune was to have worked with three great minds: Dr. Vikram Sarabhai of the Department of Space, Professor Satish Dhawan, who succeeded him and Dr. Brahm Prakash, the father of nuclear material. I was lucky to have worked with all three of them closely and consider this as a great opportunity of my life. I see four milestones in my career:

I spent twenty years in ISRO [Indian Space Research Organization]. I was given the opportunity to be the Project Director for India's first satellite launch vehicle, SLV3, the one that launched Rohini. These years played a very important role in my life as a Scientist.

After my ISRO years, I joined DRDO [Defence Research and Development Organization] and got a chance to be the part of India's guided missile program. It was my second bliss when Agni met its mission requirements in 1994.

The Department of Atomic Energy and DRDO had this tremendous partnership in the recent nuclear tests, on May 11 and 13. This was the third bliss. The joy of participating with my team in these nuclear tests and proving to the world that India can make it, that we are no longer a developing nation but one of them, made me feel very proud as an Indian.

We have now developed for Agni a re-entry structure, for

which we have developed this new material, a very light material called carbon-carbon. One day an orthopedic surgeon from Nizam Institute of Medical Sciences visited my laboratory. He lifted the material and found it so light that he took me to his hospital and showed me his patients. There were these little girls and boys with heavy metallic calipers weighing over three kilograms each, dragging their feet around.

He said to me, "Please remove the pain of my patients." In three weeks, we made these floor-reaction Orthosis 300-gram calipers and took them to the orthopedic center. The children didn't believe their eyes. From dragging around a three kilogram load on their legs, they could now move around! Their parents had tears in their eyes. That was my fourth bliss!

Why is the media here so negative? Why are we in India so embarrassed to recognize our own strengths, our achievements? We are such a great nation. We have so many amazing success stories but we refuse to acknowledge them. Why?

We are the first in milk production.

We are number one in remote-sensing satellites.

We are the second largest producer of wheat.

We are the second largest producer of rice.

Look at Dr. Sudarshan, he has transferred a tribal village into a self-sustaining, self-driving unit.

There are millions of such achievements but our media

is only obsessed with the bad news and failures and disasters.

I was in Tel Aviv once and I was reading the Israeli newspaper. It was the day after a lot of attacks and bombardments and deaths had taken place. The Hamas had struck. But the front page of the newspaper had a picture of a Jewish gentleman who, in five years, had transformed his desert land into an orchid and a granary. It was this inspiring picture that everyone woke up to. The gory details of killings, bombardments, deaths, were inside in the newspaper, buried among other news. In India we only read about death, sickness, terrorism, crime. Why are we so negative?

Another question: Why are we, as a nation so obsessed with foreign things? We want foreign TVs, we want foreign shirts, and we want foreign technology. Why this obsession with everything imported? Do we not realize that self-respect comes with self-reliance? I was in Hyderabad giving this lecture, when a 14 year old girl asked me for my autograph. I asked her what her goal in life is. She replied, 'I want to live in a developed India.' For her, you and I will have to build this developed India. You must proclaim. India is not an underdeveloped nation. It is a highly developed nation.

You say that our government is inefficient.

You say that our laws are too old.

You say that the municipality does not pick up the garbage.

You say that the phones don't work, the railways are a

joke, the airline is the worst in the world, the mails never reach their destination.

You say that our country has been fed to the dogs and is the absolute pits.

You say, say and say.

What do you do about it? Take a person on his way to Singapore. Give him a name – yours. Give him a face – yours. You walk out of the airport and you are at your International best.

In Singapore, you don't throw cigarette butts on the roads or eat in the stores. You are as proud of their underground links as they are. You pay $5 (approx. Rs.60) to drive through Orchard Road (equivalent of Mahim Causeway or Pedder Road) between 5 PM and 8 PM. You come back to the parking lot to punch your parking ticket if you have over stayed in a restaurant or a shopping mall, irrespective of your status identity. In Singapore you don't say anything, do you? You wouldn't dare to eat in public during Ramadan in Dubai. You would not dare to go out without your head covered in Jeddah. You would not dare to buy an employee of the telephone exchange in London at 10 pounds (Rs. 650) a month to "see to it that my STD and ISD calls are billed to someone else."

You would not dare to speed beyond 55 mph (88 km/h) in Washington and then tell the traffic cop, "Jaanta hai sala main kaun hoon? (Do you know who I am?) "I am so and so's son. Take your two bucks and get lost." You wouldn't chuck an empty coconut shell anywhere other than the garbage pail on the beaches in Australia and New Zealand. Why don't you spit paan on the streets of Tokyo? Why don't you use examination jockeys or buy fake certificates in Boston? We are still talking of the same you. You, who can respect and conform to a foreign system in other countries, but cannot in your own. You, who will throw papers and cigarettes on the road the moment you touch Indian ground. If you can be an involved and appreciative citizen in an alien country, why cannot you be the same here in India?

Once in an interview, the famous ex-municipal commissioner of Bombay, Mr. Tinaikar, had a point to make. "Rich people's dogs are walked on the streets to leave their affluent droppings all over the place," he said. "And then the same people turn around to criticize and blame the authorities for inefficiency and dirty pavements. What do they expect the officers to do? Go down with a broom every time their dog feels the pressure in his bowels? In America every dog owner has to clean up after his pet has done the job, and the same is in Japan. Will the Indian citizen do that here?" He's right. We go to the polls to choose a government and after that forfeit all responsibility. We sit back wanting to be pampered and expect the government to do everything for us whilst our contribution is totally negative. We expect the government to clean up but we are not going to stop chucking garbage all over the place nor are we going to stop to pick up a stray piece of paper and throw it in the bin. We expect the railways to provide clean bathrooms but we are not going to learn the proper use of bathrooms.

We want Indian Airlines and Air India to provide the best of food and toiletries but we are not going to stop pilfering at the least opportunity. This applies even to the staff who is known not to pass on the service to the public. When it comes to burning social issues like those related to women, dowry, girl child and others, we make loud drawing room protestations and continue to do the reverse at home. Our excuse? "It's the whole system which has to change, how will it matter if I alone forego my sons' rights to a dowry."

So who's going to change the system? What does a system consist of? Very conveniently for us it consists of our neighbors, other households, other cities, other communities and the government, but definitely not me and you. When it comes to actually making a positive contribution to the system, we lock ourselves along with our families into a safe cocoon and look into the distance at countries far away and wait for a Mr. Clean to come along and work miracles for us with a majestic sweep of his hand or we leave the country and run away. Like lazy cowards hounded by our fears, we run to America to bask in their glory and praise their system. When New York becomes insecure, we run to England. When England experiences unemployment, we take the next flight out to the Gulf. When the Gulf is war struck, we demand to be rescued and brought home by the Indian government.

Everybody is out to abuse and rape the country. Nobody thinks of feeding the system. Our conscience is mortgaged to money.

Dear Indians,

I am echoing J. F. Kennedy's words to his fellow Americans to relate to Indians: "Ask what we can do for India and do what has to be done to make India what America and other western countries are today."

Let's do what India needs from us.

Thank you

ABHINAV BINDRA

2013

GoSports Foundation Conclave

Indian shooter and World champion in air-rifle shooting, Abhinav Singh Bindra is an accomplished sportsperson. He was the first Indian to bag the gold medal individually in the Men's 10 meter air-rifle event at 2008 Beijing Olympic Games. He has been bringing laurels to the country since 1995, when he first won the Ropar District Shooting Championship. He has also won a number of medals in other, distinguished international events. Honoured with the Arjuna Award in 2000 at the young age of 17, Abhinav Bindra is also among the younger recipients of the prestigious Rajiv Gandhi Khel Ratna Award in 2001.

At the GoSports Foundation Athletes' Conclave on July 17, 2013, Abhinav Bindra in his speech shared his determined journey as a shooter. The story of his transformation from a geeky, lazy boy into a focused shooter making records for the country is really inspiring. With his frank words, Abhinav openly discussed the fears that haunted him, the human instincts and emotions from each win and loss, the confusion and burden of expectation. Taking examples from his personal life, he also mentioned the things that hurt, also sharing his learning experiences and how he eventually understood the game, and himself, better.

Known for his sharp aim at the bull's eye, Abhinav shares the secrets of his focus. The most important of all, he says, is to have clearly defined goals. If you don't know what you're looking for, you'll most certainly feel lost, and so he emphasises the fact using his own examples. Delivered to a young audience of sportspeople, this speech struck many chords with its simplicity, honesty and praiseworthy determination.

GoSports Foundation Conclave, 2013

Good morning ladies and gentlemen.

Think of a boy. The youngest in the family, adored and indulged by his parents and older sister; a mama's boy. I used to be that boy. Picture me when I was 9 years old. A normal boy who liked goofing off with friends, didn't like reading and hated physical activity. I think I worked hardest at bunking PE classes at school. See me as I was then. Fat and wearing glasses, because I was short-sighted. Everything was perfect. Except that my dad kept pushing me, saying, "Try sport." I tried cricket and football, but I hated the exertion, and my heart wasn't in it.

Like most boys, I loved the idea of guns – the power, the 'bang-bang' noise. One Sunday, as my dad was cleaning his three guns, I thought: 'Maybe I should try shooting as a sport. At least I won't have to run around.' That's how it began. So how does a boy who is neither talented nor athletic win the Olympic gold?

Friends, there are a thousand ways to be successful, and I am nobody to tell you the way that is right for you. No one can do that. Each one of us has to find our own path, the way that works best for us. At the same time, I welcome the opportunity to share with you some of my experiences, and hope that they will help you find your individual path in your journey to success. Because you know, no matter how many people support you and help you, when you perform, you are alone.

Some of what I'm sharing are things I wish someone had said to me when I was your age – hungry, desperate, eager to win; my whole life staked on each competition. So how does a boy who is neither talented nor athletic become both World and Olympic champion? The answer is a four-letter word; in fact, it is two four-letter words: Hard Work.

I was tenacious. I hung on despite disappointments. I was stubborn as a mule. I refused to give up. I believed in myself. And when my belief in myself faltered, I had the sense to listen to my team – my family and coaches – who believed in me for me. I was fortunate to be coached by Lt. Col. Dhillon, a taskmaster of the old school. Every day, he seemed to be waiting for me to come late for practice, or take short-cuts, or give up, or go home early, disheartened by my performance that day. Every day, he seemed to wait for me to begin complaining, like the spoilt boy he believed I was.

I was determined never to give him the satisfaction of having his expectations fulfilled. Every day he waited in vain. Till he suddenly shifted his expectations of me, and began enrolling me in shooting competitions.

Meanwhile, I was undergoing a transformation of another sort. What began as bloody-mindedness – I would never give the Colonel the satisfaction that I gave up or gave in – ended in seduction. I was seduced by the call of the bullseye.

One tiny dot that called to me over and over again, saying, "Come and get me." And I followed the call gladly, willingly.

Of course I paid the price for following my passion. My friends faded away. It was such an alien sport – shooting. Nobody knew anything about it. Had it been cricket, I'd have kept my friends – maybe our friendship might even have been strengthened. But with shooting, there was no chance. A gun and a target don't allow talk – not even encouraging talk.

You must understand that those days, children lived very different lives. You went to school, came home, played outside with your friends, and got back home. There were no malls at which you could hang out, so I just kept on going to school and shooting every afternoon. My mother managed my schedule with military precision, and life was full.

I was still 13 when I saw the wonderful Jaspal Rana at the 1996 Olympics in Atlanta. My sister swears I told her then that I would win an Olympic gold for India.

For the first time in my life, I had dedicated myself, committed myself to something, and as I spent more and more time shooting, I found myself fascinated by the sport.

In the beginning, obviously, I wanted to maximize my score. I had one, single focus – hit as many shots as I can into the very centre of the bullseye. But as I got better, I found that just a great score alone did not make me feel good.

You know – you are athletes – some days seem to be charmed. You're not making any special effort, but you're breaking records in training. Your action is so smooth that you might well be gliding on air. Everything goes right. But there's a 'But' in your head and your heart.

You know that this is just a lucky chance – you can neither predict nor control when it will happen again. In fact, it may never happen again. So what good is a 'lucky' performance? Not much good.

I wish someone had told me that more than getting the perfect score, what would give me satisfaction, what would give me a sense of achievement as an athlete, was when I knew that this score came from my effort – from something I had done – rather than because I was having a lucky day.

It shocked me – shooting 600/600 and feeling lousy. I thought to myself: If even winning is not enough, then what is it I'm trying to do here?

And I groped my way forward, to find another goal to focus on. Now what I wanted was: to win and feel good about winning.

Friends, this is a point in your path you may already have reached. I want to assure you that dissatisfaction with perfect scores is normal. Because you know that in reality, you will be competing against a whole bunch of very talented, skilled practitioners of your sport. And you need more than luck to get you the gold you want.

And so there is this strange feeling: I may feel better about shooting 594/600 than 597/600. Because 594 was my effort, and 597 was a lucky chance.

In those days, there was no organization or system that exposed athletes to the facilities, training, and equipment of sport in the international arena. You, dear friends, are in a fortunate position in comparison. Organizations such as the GoSports Foundation are committed to your welfare, working actively to ensure young athletes with world-class potential receive all the support, knowledge and encouragement necessary to empower them to achieve their dreams.

I attended shooting camps in Germany where I shot against the best marksmen, and saw no shame in losing to them. Instead, I learned. It helped that I was a boy, and awestruck at shooting alongside such illustrious people.

But this itself became a problem. If you look up to someone, you can never seriously compete against them. Think about it. If you find yourself in a swimming competition against Michael Phelps, would you really be able to put your heart and soul into beating him? Even if you did try, in your heart of hearts, do you really believe you could beat him?

I wish someone had told me that it's not always about how good you are and how hard you work and how much practice you put in. You need to be mentally tough. Even if you have to shoot against the person you most admire, you have to be able to put that admiration aside. Otherwise, you might as well not compete. Because you have already lost this competition in your mind.

My Swiss-German coaches Gaby Buehlmann and Heinz

Reinkemeier saw my 'niceness' as a major hurdle in my ability to win matches. Now I don't think I'm so much nicer than the average person. I am a regular, gentle, polite person. But regular, gentle and polite does not win matches. I needed 'killer instinct', 'me vs. you all' type of mental toughness. Today many people misunderstand it for arrogance or aloofness. But it was a shield I developed against people because I had to develop it if I wanted to have a serious shot at winning my dreams.

I wish someone had told me that I would be misunderstood by so many people as I worked to attain a quest that would make us all proud. It hurt – it hurt then and it hurts now. Only now, it doesn't hurt as much, because you get used to things; you don't let them affect you as much.

I have always been a diligent student. No detail is too small to interest me. I want to know everything about everything that has to do with shooting. Even today, when I do know a few things, I keep looking for new things to learn to get better – always better. I may never be perfect. That's okay. But I can always be better than I was yesterday.

My next challenge was clear – how could I get better? Yes, it's the same old thing – hard work. But instead of just aiming my rifle at the bull's-eye and reading my score, I began to look at other things: improving my technique, customizing my equipment, learning more about myself, and so on.

Was my body comfortable when I sank into my stance to shoot? When I became tired, it was harder to shoot well. Alright, so I have to find ways to delay the tiredness. Maybe I should train my muscles to be stronger, so they won't get tired so quickly. And so, ironically, I began working hard at working out, because I wanted my body to cope better with muscle strain and fatigue, because I wanted to get better results; because I wanted to win.

Are there pellets which can improve my shooting accuracy? Research, find out, experiment. Go deeper. When I see that I'm close to a perfect score, my heart starts hammering in excitement, anticipating that perfect result. Do I spoil the last shot because I'm too excited? Yes, I do. Okay, I have to find a way to be less excited.

I'd like to emphasize that I did all this at various times in my life to break out of stuck situations, but always, whether I was stuck or not, whether I was winning or losing, what I followed rigorously – almost religiously – was my training. I never compromised. One day, I was doing crunches in reps of 10. My trainer said, "Good job, 10 done." There's nobody there to check, the trainer has counted 10, but I know it is 8, so I said, "No. It was 8, not 10." And then I do two more to make it 10.

When people ask me what helped me win gold, this is what I say to them. "I slogged my guts out – I did it without compromise, when there was no one to see, no one to be impressed. I did it when I did not feel like it. And the reason I did it is because my desire to win was, and is, much greater than my desire to make excuses or find reasons not to win.

I wish someone had told me that no matter how hard you work, how dedicatedly, how much you push yourself, you will not always win. And you have to learn to pick up the broken pieces of yourself after you lose, knit yourself back together again, and start the process all over again. It is impossible that you will win everything all the time. Even in his prime, the supreme athlete Roger Federer, did lose some matches. So you need to think about and prepare yourself for failure as well. Because it will come, as surely as night follows day.

I was 17 when a wild card entry, called a hardship quota in shooting, allowed me to participate at the Sydney Olympics in 2000. I think that is when I understood the range and depth and height of what the Olympic Games mean to a sportsperson. Once in 4 years, you get the chance to shoot the best you can for 2 hours. That's it. If you haven't done it then, you begin all over again, preparing for the 2 hours you want to get after 4 years, in the next Olympics. My ambition solidified. This time around, I was an inexperienced shooter. Next time, I would be ready.

I wish someone had told me that winning at sport was about so much more than sport. For instance, I needed to be able to deal with my luggage getting lost – when I needed my equipment to train for a competition. Once I had to wait at the airport for hours, because someone forgot to reserve a hotel room, and I was literally stranded in another country with nowhere to go until the organizers booked me a hotel room. I had to be able to get over this so that it would not affect my mood, my state of mind as I went into the competition. I needed to focus.

I wish someone had told me that I wouldn't always get home-cooked food, and might have to make do with food that was unappetizing and much lower in nutrition than I was used to – on the eve of international events. I learned all this the hard way. By going hungry, not eating enough, getting upset tummies. You know that feeling of nervousness of 'getting butterflies in your tummy.' Well, I for one, have had butterflies, goats, elephants and the odd dinosaur or two in my tummy. But I have had to ignore all these creatures and prepare to shoot my best. Sometimes on a glass of milk.

But your desire to win, to achieve your goal has to be big enough, strong enough to overcome any such hurdles you face. And frankly, the win that you struggle for is the win that you are proud of. If the win comes too easily, you are always left with a feeling of doubt: was it really me? Am I really good enough? And the taste of victory turns to ashes in your mouth.

The year 2004, in Athens at The Olympic Games, I had done everything I could to prepare myself. Many people believed I had a good chance of winning the gold. I don't win the gold. I don't win any medals. In fact, I came seventh.

I wish someone had told me that winning at sport was about so much more than sport. Days later, I find out that the tile beneath my shooting position, Position No. 3, was wobbly, and that everyone who shot from that position performed considerably worse than they were expected to.

Do the reasons really matter when your mind and spirit have been shattered? Months later, when I became capable of thinking again, my only thought was to give up shooting. I put away my equipment and immersed myself in viewing, collecting and painting art.

I did not lose focus. I gave it up. What was the point of

focusing if any arbitrary event could throw off years and years of focus and work? I lost faith in myself, in shooting as the right way of life for myself.

My coaches, my family and friends – they all walked the tightrope between giving me the time and space to heal, jollying me along, and giving me stern 'put-the-past-behind-you-and-pick-up-the-gun' talks.

More than a year later, my spirit began to stir feebly. The 2006 World Championships were a pain in the back, literally. My muscles and core were not sufficiently developed to support the long periods of time I spent in my stance. Shooters stand with their hips thrown out, and their vertebrae go through severe punishment. I invested myself in a deeper study of the body, doing weights, Pilates, strengthening my core and increasing my cardio-vascular fitness. I had also got back to my old holy grail, technique.

I had learnt that success was a fickle mistress. I decided to pursue excellence. Focus on excellence. Soldier on.

In 2006 at the world championships in Zagreb, I won the gold. This win created some good feelings and somewhat restored my faith in my abilities. But I did not lose sight of my goal – the Olympic gold. Continuing to focus on excellence, on every detail from my shoes to my clothes to the angles at which I stood, held my gun, and so on, I trained my body. You need to repeat something at least 10,000 times to make it a habit, I believe. And if you've practiced maybe 100,000 times or 1 million or 10 million times, your muscles develop a memory of your movement. This is the beginning of command, of mastery – over your sport and your body.

As the Beijing Olympics of 2008 approached, I knew I had to plan my strategy very carefully. The enemy was within me. My enemy was my mind. I needed to develop the mental strength to take the pressure of competition in my stride; not to let it affect my performance. But I had prepared for this. I had practiced keeping a calm, clear mind and reducing the voice in my head worrying about how I was doing, and what my score was, and how others were shooting, and a hundred other things. I had trained myself to mute this voice.

Okay. Game time.

I won. And the world erupted. Months later, after a whirlwind of congratulations and celebrations, I was left feeling like an open bottle of Coke. Flat, no fizz and stale.

I wish someone had told me that in some ways, winning was harder than losing. Because when you lose, you still have your goal – you simply need to take a break to process your emotions, refocus yourself and work towards achieving your goal. But when you win, you lose your goal. Where now, will you find the motivation to work when you've already achieved your dream? 10 crunches? 5 are enough. No. Wait a minute, why do any crunches at all? Why train?

A peculiar lack of energy, of drive, took hold of me. I found myself drifting. I wish someone had told me that after I had won, I would need to find goals beyond winning. Those were dark days too, because I was petrified. If I didn't want to shoot, what would I do with the rest of my life? Shooting is all

I knew!

Obviously, I had to keep participating in competitions, but I didn't win anything.

We Indians are a warm-hearted people. We are a whole-hearted people. We either love or hate. There is nothing between the two extremes. Everyone loved me after I won in Beijing. But oh, how they hated me when I did not continue my winning spree. I wish someone had told me how each doubt cast at my ability to win would be like a fresh dart thrown at my already-wounded self. Even though I thought I had developed a thick hide, and did not care much about what people thought or said, I cared passionately, and I suffered.

My coaches were prepared for my post-victory depression. Raging controversies added insult to injury – the medal was won, what more did they want? - I withdrew into myself to find the sustenance to keep me going. The Vipassana course I did, for instance, showed me clearly that I still felt passionately about shooting.

In subsequent world championships, I did not bring home any medals. I was working hard on my technique and myself, but I had not yet dug deep enough inside, not yet found a reason I wanted badly enough to win. Till I found it: to be the only person to win the Olympic gold in air-rifle shooting twice in a row.

And then, London. "Will he repeat his feat?" The thought was deafening in its volume, even when it was not voiced. I am prepared – fully, in every way. I have foreseen and prepared for every kind of eventuality. I know this, and it strengthens my resolve to win.

Of course it didn't happen. Life is always throwing you new curve balls. By this time, shooting has been firmly established as a spectator sport, and the noise from the spectators is – literally – deafening. And I'm supposed to shut them out and shoot to win… I didn't.

I wish someone had told me that not every loss feels earth-shattering.

How differently I handled the aftermath of this not-win! I was calm – disappointed, but calm. No end-of-the-world scenarios were playing out in my mind. When one journalist asked me if I planned to retire, I replied, "I might look old, but actually, I'm pretty young." He withdrew, bemused.

I'm back home in Chandigarh, training, shooting. I'm travelling to shoot in other events all over the world. I've found a quiet confidence, an excited hum within me as I prepare for Rio in 2016. I am focusing again.

Somewhere, in a corner of my mind, I sometimes think: at least I've got this focus thing right. First, I need something to focus on. Secondly, what I focus on will keep shifting, depending on what happens in my life, and in my head. I have never been more committed to my sport, and as I explore it more deeply, I also get to know myself better – what motivates me, what excites me, what keeps me going, what I am indifferent to.

I wanted to quit shooting after Beijing, not imagining what more I could aspire to. But I dug deep and found the courage to put myself on the line. So I put myself on the line and I failed – but failure only brings out my defiant streak, pushes me to be even better, to see what else I can find inside myself.

The London Olympics were a failure as far as the result was concerned, but I count it as one of the victories in my journey of growing as a sportsperson. I am learning more, getting better, readying myself for Rio in 2016.

Today, I know there will be roadblocks, but the only way is around them. And I am determined to find a way, a solution to overcome them. I have dug my feet in the ground and decided that victory is mine. When the next win will come, I don't know. But victory is more than winning.

Victory is my relentless pursuit of excellence, victory is my commitment to my sport, victory is never giving up, never losing sight of my goal. Victory is knowing that I will do whatever it takes to get better.

I would like to close by telling you about my heroes. I don't know their names. They are the ones who work quietly, tirelessly, training whether or not they have facilities, equipment, or support. They may win medals – district-level, zonal, national, international – or they may not win anything. They show up every day when they aren't feeling well, when they're disheartened, when it's bad weather – they triumph over every circumstance to show up and train. Alone and driven by the spark that lights a fire in them, and propels them 'Faster, Higher, Stronger'.

And in that they are already victorious. Their medals will come. If not at this event, then next time.

Till next time, my friends, our next time – yours and mine…

Thank you for listening.

SHAHRUKH KHAN

2013

Courage in Success

Perhaps one of the most popular Indian actor, producer and Bollywood personality, Shahrukh Khan is famously called the 'King Khan' of the Indian movie industry. His work in Bollywood includes appearing in over 50 films ranging from action to romance to comedy, and has led him to numerous achievements. He has bagged fourteen Filmfare Awards and the Padma Shri award by the Government of India in 2005. Considered to be among the biggest stars in the history of cinema, he has been described as "the world's biggest movie star" by the Los Angeles Times.

He is the co-chairman of Red Chillies Entertainment, a motion-picture production company and also the co-owner of Kolkata Knight Riders, the Indian Premier League cricket team. Shahrukh has been involved in philanthropy as well, in areas of health care, relief funds and children's education, for which he has been honoured with UNESCO's Pyramide con Marni award in 2011.

Shahrukh Khan was asked to deliver a speech at the 40th Management Convention at All India Management Association (AIMA), New Delhi in September 2013. Aimed at getting successful leaders to talk about a topical theme of national importance, the convention endeavours to help corporate understand the industry and trends, while also enabling them to better manage key strategies for successful business performance.

Named the richest actor in the world in 2014, Shahrukh in his speech speaks of poverty and failure and how the fear of poverty kept him going and was an integral component to his future success. He provides instances from his own childhood and career and goes on to enlist the learning he generated from his experience of the industry and the world.

Good evening everyone. Let me say it at the outset: It's really scary here! The biggest managers of the biggest corporations in the biggest convention for management: AIMA. Really, it's a sad reflection that in such an august company of people and such a collection of skill set and big business houses and managers, all you could manage was to get a speaker from Bollywood to speak at the convention. Economy must really be bad.

But who am I to speak about the economical downtrend across the globe, or anything else for that matter? Just reading the topics being discussed before I came on stage, I was frightened and couldn't understand a word.

Could financialization of commodities be used to incentivise supply growth without inflating prices? Yes if u say so, or no if you are in a bad mood, sir. Managing liquidity, supply crunch, risk of NPA, CSR mandate, CEOs, COOs, CFOs, UFOs, mind boggling and numbing for a person like me, who can just about say 'kkkkcorporate' management without falling over his own shoelaces. And I have to speak about courage in this scared and ill-informed mindset of mine.

But here I am and so are all of you wonderful people. I wish you a great convention and a happy economy, and I want to thank my friend Shiv for giving me this opportunity to speak in front of such an extraordinary amazement of grey matter, all you highly successful, perhaps the most successful people in the world, and give a speech on success!

Am I the only one who is seeing this irony or are you all too busy holding back your laughter as to what I will say here? Apart from my lack of knowledge and fear, the only other problem is that I am really not good at giving discourses on how to be successful. I am not good at this because I don't really know what I can say to you highly motivated people that you don't already know, about life, business and success.

So I will bore you with a few details of my life and how I got to be a movie star and mainly talk about success and how it came to be. Let me forewarn you, this is a recycled speech. Whenever I am called to give speeches such a big organisation, I use this speech. It's generic, simple and makes me give no commitment in our first meeting. Somewhat like the corporate world itself.

The biggest problem with success is that any narrative of success is bound to be at least a little bit dull, because it is not your story. I have sat down with people who tell me their stories of success, and I am like, 'Man! Get the hell out of my sight. If I want to feel jealous, I will see some other actor's successful film. I don't need the story of your life. Second, and more importantly so, successful people are almost never able to pinpoint what it was that made them so.

Take Warren Buffet. Here's a guy who must get asked five times a day as to how he became the most successful investor of his era. His answers — "Reinvest your profits," "Limit what you borrow," etc — are no different from what any fool could tell you. Buffet isn't being cagey. He simply doesn't know. Success is a wonderful thing, but it tends not to be the sort of experience that we learn from. We enjoy it, perhaps we even deserve it. But we don't acquire wisdom from it. And maybe that's why it cannot be passed on either. Me being successful does not mean my children will also be so, however much I teach them about what all I did in my life and even if they follow it to the letter. Success just happens. Really.

So talking about how to become successful is a waste of time. Instead let me tell you very honestly, whatever happened to me happened because I am really scared of failure. I don't want as much to succeed as much as I don't want to fail. I come from a very normal lower middle class family, and I saw a lot of failure. My father was a beautiful man, and the most successful failure in the world. My mom also failed to stay with me long enough for her to see me become a movie star. We were quite poor actually at certain junctures of our lives, and I have even experienced a kurkee, where they throw you and your belongings on the roads. Let me tell you, poverty is not an ennobling experience at all. Poverty entails fear and stress and sometimes depression; I had seen my parents go through it many times. It means a thousand petty humiliations and hardships. At an early age after my parents died, I equated poverty with failure. I just didn't want to be poor, so when I got a chance to act in films, it wasn't out of any creative desire that I signed my films. It was just purely out of the fear of

failure and poverty that I signed most of my initial films. Most of them were discards of actors and the producers could not find anyone else to do them.

Deewana was discarded by Armaan Kohli, Baazigar was rejected by Salman Khan and Darr was negated by Aamir Khan. I did them all for just making sure that I was working to avoid unemployment. The timing or something was right, and that made them happen and I became a big star. I asked Dilip Kumar sahib once, that why he did Devdas, and he looked at me and said, for the money yaar. Bimalda paid me one lakh rupees. I didn't know it would be such a great film and make me such a huge actor. That's the only reason I did Devdas, which means sometimes our success is not the direct result of our actions. It just happens on its own and we take credit for it, out of embarrassment sometimes.

So I believe the true road to success is not just the desire for success but a fear of failure. I tell everyone if you don't enjoy and be scared of your failure hard enough, you will never succeed. I am not going to stand here and tell you that failure is fun, but I will insist and hope that all of us should experience failure in some measure. The extent of what each one of us perceives as failure may differ, as it should, but I believe one needs to pass through some stages of failure if they really want to succeed.

So how does failure help us?

First and foremost, it's not the absence of failure that makes you a success. It is your response to failure that actually helps to buffer the reverses that you experience. I for one, have two responses to failure. The first is pragmatism, a recognition and belief that if one approach does not work then the other will or might. The second response is fatalism. I fool myself that it was bound to happen and I need to move on, not get caught up in the often repeated question, God why does it happen to me?

Second, failure also gives me an incentive to greater exertion, harder work, which invariably leads to later success in most cases.

Third, failure is an amazing teacher. If you don't fail, you will never learn. And if you don't learn, you will never grow. There is a well-known story of a bank president who was asked the secret of his success. "Right decisions," he replied. "How do you get to know how to make right decisions?" came the follow-up question. "Experience," was the answer. "Well, how do you get experience?" asked his interrogator. "Wrong decisions," he replied.

Fourth, sometimes it has taught me to stop pretending that I am someone else than what I am supposed to be. It gives me a clear cut direction that hey, maybe I am not supposed to be doing this. Let me just concentrate on finishing and doing things that really matter to me, that define me, instead of following a particular course that actually is taking me away from what really my core liking is. KKR my cricket team is one such example. Through the advice of my friends like Shiv, I took on a CEO and a whole new department that would handle the job better.

Fifth, failure also gets you to find who your real friends are. The true strength of your relationships only gets tested in the face of strong adversity. I lost lots of friends post Ra.One, apart from losing lots of audience too and then post Chennai Express, I am happy to tell you that though I haven't made any new friends, I have a whole new set of enemies.

Sixth, regular failures also have taught me empathy towards others. Being a star, it is easy to be prone to the notion that I am superior, self-sufficient and fantastic, instead of realizing that I was just plain lucky or got some lucky breaks.

Seventh, overcoming some of my failure has made me discover that I have a strong will, and more discipline than I suspected. It has helped me have confidence in my ability to survive.

So all in all I think failure is a good thing. I won't bore you with more details of how failure is a good thing, because then you will not call me back again for a talk on success and such, the next time. But I would like to tell you all that life is a not just a check-list of acquisitions, attainments and fulfilments. Your qualifications and CV don't really matter. Jobs don't matter. Instead life is difficult and complicated, and beyond anyone's control and the humility to know that by respecting your failures will help you survive its vicissitudes.

There is the greatest practical benefit in making a few failures in life. I say making because failure is not an exterior force, I believe it happens due to our own actions and reactions, in such convoluted ways that we may not understand, but we are the reason for it. So don't be weighed down by it, cherish the experience and learn from it. By experiencing all and accepting it, you will experience success, not in isolation of life's full offerings.

Let me conclude by saying that my hope for you is a

lifelong love of learning, exciting and Inspiring dreams, businesses, profits, deals, power lunches or whatever turns you guys and girls on but alongside I wish you a fair number of moderate failures too. By experiencing all, I hope that you will experience success.

Success is never final, just like failure is never fatal. Courage is ill-defined if we think it is doing something macho, risky or chancy. If that happens at somebody else's cost, it's even less courageous. Courage is doing what you are afraid to do, personally scared to do in whichever capacity you work. There can be no courage unless you are scared. So be scared, in order to feel the courage. Be fearful. I believe one has to have the fear of failure so much, that you get the courage to succeed.

So that's my learned piece on courage in success. Or what I call 'The Success of Failure' and being scared enough to be courageous, to make it so.

Or if I was to put it in the words that surrounded me and those that I was scared of, when I entered this august gathering: The theory of the management of high rising failure works to convert failure into success by a growth index of 100 percent, while understanding the indices of fear and not compromising the syntax of our courage globally, while keeping a holistic 360 degree view of our domestic market through rigorous system and processes.

In simple terms or in film language, it means, if at first you don't succeed, reload and try again. Shoot fast, shoot first and be ready to take a bullet too. Remember what Don said, Iss company ki management ke dushman ki sabse badi galati yeh hai, ki woh iss company ka dushman hai, kyunki jab tak dushman apni pehli chaal chalta hai, yeh company apni agli chaal chal chuki hoti hai.

Thank you very much.

SACHIN TENDULKAR

2013

A Farewell to Cricket

Bidding farewell to a phenomenal cricket career, Indian sports-star Sachin Tendulkar gave a heart-warming speech after his final match. His 200th and final test match before complete retirement from cricket was held against the West Indies in Mumbai's Wankhede Stadium on November 16, 2013. As soon as the match ended, announcing India's win, the entire Indian cricket team gave Sachin a much-deserved, moving lap of honour.

Fondly called 'Master Blaster', Sachin has numerous records to his credit and is considered the most 'complete' batsman in cricket. He has scored more than 30,000 runs in all forms of international cricket (Tests, ODIs and Twenty20 Internationals) and is the only player to have achieved this feat. Sachin also holds records for having the highest number of centuries in both Tests (51) and ODIs (49) and similar other records in the game. He has been the recipient of National Awards and Honours, such as the Arjuna Award in 1994, Rajiv Gandhi Khel Ratna Award in 1997-98, Padhma Shri in 1999, Padhma Vibhushan in 2008 and the Bharat Ratna, India's highest civilian award in 2014.

In his farewell speech, he displayed heart-felt gratitude, thanking everyone who had a role in making his career a success: his parents, siblings, wife and children, friends, coaches, doctors, team-mates and all his well-wishers. He spoke about cricket and how it shaped his life, recounting his journey with sentiment in this twenty-minute speech, while thousands of fans and well-wishers witnessed this emotional moment. Sachin is considered a legend across various generations, having inspired millions of Indians with his apparent dedication, humility and talent.

All my friends, settle down, let me talk, I will get more and more emotional. My life between 22 yards for 24 years, it is hard to believe that that wonderful journey has come to an end. But I would like to take this opportunity to thank people who have played an important role in my life. Also for the first time in my life, I am carrying this list, to remember all the names in case I forget someone. I hope you understand. It's getting a little bit difficult to talk, but I will manage.

The most important person in my life, and I have missed him a lot since 1999 when he passed away, was my father. Without his guidance, I don't think I would have been standing here in front of you. He gave me freedom at the age of 11, when he told me that [I should] chase my dreams, but make sure you do not find short cuts. The path might be difficult, but don't give up, and I have simply followed his instructions. Above all, he told me to be a nice human being, which I will continue to try to be, and try my best. Every time I have done something special [and] showed my bat, it was for my father.

My mother, I don't know how she dealt with such a naughty child like me. I was not easy to manage. She must be extremely patient. For a mother, the most important thing is that her child remains safe and healthy and fit. That was what she was most bothered and worried about. She has taken care of me for these past 24 years that I have played for India, but even before that, she started praying for me the day I started playing cricket. She just prayed and prayed and I think her prayers and blessings have given me the strength to go out and perform. So a big thank you to my mother for all the sacrifices.

In my school days, for four years, I stayed with my uncle and aunt because my school was quite far from my home, and they treated me like their son. After a hard day's play, I would be half-asleep, and my aunt would be feeding me food so I could go again and play the next day. I can't forget these moments. I am like their son and I am glad it has continued to be the same way.

My eldest brother Nitin and his family have always encouraged me. My eldest brother doesn't like to talk much, but the one thing he always told me is, 'Whatever you do, I know you will always give it 100 percent, and I have full faith and confidence in you'. His encouragement meant a lot to me. My sister Savita and her family, was no different. The first cricket bat of my life was presented to me by my sister. It was a Kashmir willow bat. But that is where the journey began. She is one of those many who still continue to fast when I bat. So thank you very much.

Ajit, my brother, now what do I talk about him? I don't know. We have lived this dream together. He was the one who sacrificed his career for my cricket. He spotted the spark in me. And it all started from the age of 11 when he took me to [Ramakant] Achrekar Sir, my coach, and from there on my life changed. You will find this hard to believe but even last night he called up to discuss my dismissal, knowing that there was a remote chance of batting again, but the habit we have developed, the rapport we have developed since my birth, has continued and it will continue. Maybe when I'm not playing cricket we will still be discussing technique.

Various things we agreed upon: my technique, and so many technical things on which I didn't agree with him. We have had arguments and disagreements, but when I look back at all these things in my life, I would have been a lesser cricketer.

The most beautiful thing happened to me in 1990 when I met my wife Anjali. Those were special years and it has continued and will always continue that way. I know Anjali, being a doctor, there was a wonderful career in front of her. When we decided to have a family, Anjali took the initiative to step back and say that you continue with your cricket and I will take the responsibility of the family.

Without that I don't think I would have been able to play cricket freely and without stress. Thanks for bearing with all my fuss and all my frustrations, and all sorts of rubbish that I have spoken. Thanks for bearing with me and always staying by my side through all the ups and downs. You are the best partnership I've had in my life.

Then the two precious diamonds of my life, Sara and Arjun. They have already grown up. My daughter is 16, my son is 14. Time has flown by. I wanted to spend so much time with them on special occasions like their birthdays, their annual days, their sports days, going on holidays, whatever. I have missed out on all those things. Thanks for your understanding. Both of you have been so, so special to me you cannot imagine. I promise you that for 14 and 16 years I have not spent enough time with both of you, but the next 16 years or even beyond that, everything is for you.

My in-laws, Anand Mehta and Annabelle, both have been so, so supportive [and] loving and caring. I have discussed various things in life generally with them, and have taken their advice. You know, it's so important to have a strong family who is always with you and who are guiding you. Before you start clapping, the most important thing they did was allowing me to marry Anjali. So thank you very much.

In the past 24 years that I have played for India, I have made new friends, and before that I have had friends from my childhood. They have all had a terrific contribution. As and when I have called them to come and bowl to me at the nets, they have left their work aside to come and help me. Be it joining me on holidays and having discussions with me on cricket, or when I was a little stressed and wanting to find a solution so I could perform better.

All those moments my friends were with me. When I was injured, I would wake up in the morning because I couldn't sleep and thought that my career was over because of injuries, that is when my friends have woken up at 3 o'clock in the morning to drive with me and make me believe that my career was not over. Life would be incomplete without all those friends. Thanks for being there for me.

My cricket career started when I was 11. The turning point of my career was when my brother (Ajit) took me to Achrekar Sir. I was extremely delighted to see him up in the stands. Normally he sits in front of the television and he watches all the games that I play. When I was 11 or 12, those were the days when I used to hop back on his scooter and play a couple of practice matches a day. The first half of the innings I would be batting at Shivaji Park, the second half at some other match in Azad Maidan. He would take me all over Mumbai to make sure I got match practice.

On a lighter note, in the last 29 years, Sir has never ever said 'well played' to me because he thought I would get complacent and I would stop working hard. Maybe he can push his luck and wish me now, well done on my career, because there are no more matches, Sir, in my life. I will be witnessing cricket, and cricket will always stay in my heart, but you have had an immense contribution in my life. So thank you very much.

My cricket for Mumbai started right here on this ground, the Mumbai Cricket Association (MCA). I remember landing from New Zealand at 4 o'clock in the morning and turning up for a game here at 8 o'clock just because I wanted to be a part of Mumbai cricket, not that somebody forced me. That was for the love of Mumbai cricket. The president is here, so thank you very much, along with your team, for taking care of me and looking after my cricket.

The dream was obviously to play for India, and that is where my association with the BCCI started. The BCCI was fantastic, right from my debut, they believed in my ability and selecting me into the squad at the age of 16 was a big step. So thanks to all the selectors for having faith in me and the BCCI for giving me the freedom to express myself out in the middle. Things would have been different if you had not been behind me, and I really appreciate your support. Especially when I was injured, you were right with me and making sure that all the treatments were taken care of, and that I got fit and fine and playing [right] back for India.

The journey has been special. The last 24 years I have played with many senior cricketers, and even before that there were many senior cricketers whom I watched on television. They inspired me to play cricket, and to play in the right way. Thanks to all those senior cricketers, and unfortunately I have not been able to play with them, but I have high regard for all their achievements and all their contributions.

We see it on the mega-screen, Rahul, Laxman, Sourav and Anil, who is not here, and my team-mates right here in front me. You are like my family away from home. I have had some wonderful times with you. It is going to be difficult to not be part of the dressing room, sharing those special moments. All the coaches for their guidance, it has been special for me.

When M.S. Dhoni presented me the 200th Test match cap on Day One morning, I had a brief message for the team. I would like to repeat that. I just feel that all of us are so, so fortunate and proud to be part of the Indian cricket team and serving the nation. Knowing all of you guys, I know you will continue to serve the nation in the right spirit and right values. I believe we have been the lucky ones to be chosen by the Almighty to serve this sport. Each generation gets this opportunity to take care of this sport and serve it to the best of our ability. I have full faith in you to continue to serve the nation in the right spirit and to the best of your ability, to bring all the laurels to the country. All the very best.

I would be failing in my duties if I did not thank all the doctors, the physios, the trainers who have put this difficult body together to go back on the field and be able to play. The amount of injuries that I have had in my career, I don't know how you have managed to keep me fit, but without your special efforts, it would never have happened. The doctors have met me at weird hours. I have called them from Mumbai to Chennai, Mumbai to Delhi, I mean wherever. They have just taken the next flight and left their work and families to be with me, which has allowed me to play. So a big thank you to all three of you for keeping me in good shape.

My dear friend, late Mark Mascarenhas, my first manager. We unfortunately lost him in a car accident in 2001, but he was such a well-wisher of cricket, my cricket, and especially Indian cricket. He was so passionate. He understood what it takes to represent a nation and gave me all the space to go out and express myself, and never pressured me to do this ad or promotion or whatever the sponsors demanded. He took care of that and today I miss him, so thank you Mark for all your contribution.

My current management team, WSG, for repeating what Mark has done, because when I signed the contract I told them exactly what I want from them, and what it requires to represent me. They have done that and respected that.

Someone who has worked closely with me for 14 years is my manager, Vinod Nayudu. He is more like my family and all the sacrifices, spending time away from his family for my work, has been special, so a big thank you to his family as well for giving up so much time for my work with Vinod.

In my school days, when I performed well, the media backed me a lot. They continue to do that till this morning. Thank you so much to the media for supporting and appreciating my performances. It surely had a positive effect on me. Thank you so much to all the photographers as well for those wonderfully captured moments that will stay with me for the rest of my life.

I know my speech is getting a bit too long, but this is the last thing I want to say. I want to thank all the people here who have flown in from various parts of the world, and have supported me endlessly, whether I scored a 0 or a 100-plus. Your support was so dear to me and meant a lot to me. Whatever you have done for me.

I know I have met so many guys who have fasted for me, prayed for me, done so much for me. Without that life wouldn't have been like this for me. I want to thank you from the bottom of my heart, and also say that time has flown by rather quickly, but the memories you have left with me will always be with me forever and ever, especially 'Sachin, Sachin' which will reverberate in my ears till I stop breathing. Thank you very much. If I have missed out on saying something, I hope you understand.

Goodbye.

AZIM PREMJI

2013

Lifetime Achievement Award Acceptance, Economic Times Awards

Indian business tycoon Azim Hashid Premji is the chairman of Wipro Limited, a leading giant in the Indian software industry. He is also a dedicated philanthropist, and to give shape to his strong ideas on the importance of quality education, he founded the Azim Premji Foundation in 2001. The Foundation runs as a non-profit organization to provide elementary education to disadvantaged and remote areas within the country. He has twice been listed in Time magazine's '100 most influential people' list, and is currently the fourth wealthiest Indian.

This speech was delivered by Azim Premji on December 2013 at the Economic Times awards, where he was felicitated with a Lifetime Achievement Award. He spoke about the importance of philanthropy and how his company has initiated a number of activities garnered towards the promotion of education. He talks about how actively running the Foundation has helped not just other, underprivileged people, but also been a reason of moral fulfilment for himself and his employees. Azim Premji is especially proud of the fact that his employees are utterly dedicated, and use their holidays, if required, to contribute to the Foundation's causes, travelling to villages and taking part in the many initiatives. He dispels the common notion of teachers not being interested in learning so they can teach better, for he learns from his experience, that sometimes it is the lack of resources, not the lack of motivation.

With his humble words, he displays genuine empathy for fellow humans and projects the image of the sweet fruit of morality that such causes bear. He also shells out a little guidance for future philanthropists, voiced through the valuable lessons he learned from his own experience.

Lifetime Achievement Award Acceptance,
Economic Times Awards, 2013

Good evening. It's a pleasure to be here with all of you. I want to thank the Economic Times for bestowing this honour on me. While I receive this honour, the simple fact is that it is actually an honour for the thousands of my colleagues and partners, who have helped build Wipro to what it is, over the past few decades. Thank you.

It was suggested by the Economic Times that I share some thoughts on Philanthropy on this occasion. Let's think about tonight. We will all go home or go to our hotels and sleep. No matter where we are, within a couple of kilometres of where we are sleeping safely and soundly, there will be a young girl, who is our daughters' age or our granddaughter's age, trying to sleep in the cold night of December on the roads.

She has been abused in the past, and she will be abused in the future. She is probably desperately hungry. In her circumstances, going to school or having anything else that every child must have is not even a remote possibility. When she wakes up tomorrow morning, it's just the start of another day of trying to survive, to again sleep shivering on the cold pavement somewhere.

This girl is not alone. There are probably 3 million children, who are homeless and will sleep on the streets in India tonight and every night. She is also not alone in sleeping hungry. More than 200 million of our people will probably sleep hungry, like her. In very simple terms: can we be indifferent to this?

To my mind that is the basic question that we need to ask ourselves, do we feel connected to our country, to the people around us? Should not every Indian have the very basic, very bare necessities of a life of dignity? This is certainly not hoping for too much, it is just basic safety, adequate food, a roof to sleep, basic education and healthcare.

Most of us would we feel this way, I think we just need to act.

I have mentioned only a few kinds of issues. But as all of us know that our country is facing challenges of similar kind on every front. Be it education, healthcare, nutrition, sanitation or of deep inequality and discrimination. Each one is as complex as the other, and each one as necessary for a life of basic dignity. We can perhaps justifiably say that many of these issues need to be addressed by the government. Certainly the government needs to do more and better. But that doesn't in any way lessen the responsibility that we have. I and you, who have the privilege of being successful, have a greater responsibility.

To me, philanthropy is the connection that we can have if we are not indifferent to all these issues that face us. It is the mechanism for us to contribute to making some positive change. And I think, the greater our success, the greater the responsibility for us. I must also say that the desire to engage must come from within. No one can be told to be philanthropic. At its core, philanthropy is about the connection that you feel with the people around you or the world around you. Many of those who feel this connection and have taken action, have experienced that there is enough reason for hope in our country, and that one can genuinely contribute.

The Foundation that we have set up has been working with various state governments to improve equity and quality of government schools for the past twelve years. I have learned that trying to improve education is a very long process, but I think that basic education is the basic route to building a better society, so we remain totally committed to it. Let me narrate one of many things that give us hope in this journey.

We work in some of the most disadvantaged districts of the country. We have 50-70 of our own people in each of these districts. They are all deeply committed to the cause of education, and are capable of educating teachers. In all these places we run voluntary learning forums for government school teachers, amongst many other initiatives. What this means is that teachers come to these learning sessions on their own. They spend their own money for transportation; they come from up to 30 kilometres away in difficult conditions. They also spend their own money on food. They do this on a holiday, usually a Sunday.

Can we imagine this happening in the best of the companies? How many employees of such companies will spend their holidays and their own money, so that they can do their jobs better? How completely contrary is this experience of ours, to the notion of the disinterested government employee?

These are all government employees, but they are deeply committed and they genuinely care.

Our experience has been that between 12-18% teachers in a district become a part of such forums over a period of time. And if you ask them why they do it, they all have the same answer, which is that they want to learn so that they can teach better. We are not talking about small numbers. In a typical district with 5000 teachers, this implies that 600-800 teachers are engaged in such forums.

I find this a great reason for hope. When so many people from within the government school system have this kind of commitment, I am sure education will improve, given time and sustained effort. As I said before, we have been at it for 12 years. I just have one regret about my philanthropy, which is, I wish I had started earlier. There is so much to do, and this kind of work takes so much time that the earlier we try to contribute, the better it is.

With these twelve years' of our experience, let me share three other things that I have learnt about philanthropy. Those of you who are very active in philanthropy would perhaps resonate with these lessons that I have learned:

First, involving your family early on in philanthropy is very important. Their understanding, endorsement and involvement may eventually be the most determining factor. There is another positive aspect to this early involvement. Some of the smartest people that I know have been those who chose to become home makers. They can perhaps play a significant role in starting off their families' philanthropic efforts.

Second, the key to scaling up philanthropy and doing good work is getting good people in the team. This is exactly the same as is in our businesses. The work in philanthropy is perhaps more complex than business, because social issues are more complex. So it needs really good people. I think that the most serious start to anyone's philanthropic work would be to pick one of their top people from within the business, a person who has the intent, empathy, ability, and trust and move him or her to the philanthropy side.

Third, philanthropic work needs patience, tenacity and empathy. It is different from business. We all know that intellectually, but it's very challenging when one gets into it. One has to change one's mindset significantly, if one has to make a difference. I have learned this only slowly in the past twelve years.

Thank you for hearing me out. I absolutely believe that we are trustees of our wealth for this society, and we must use it as such. We must do philanthropy because it is the right thing to do. I also believe that every one of us has the basic empathy with the people around us; we just need to let it find expression. I am certain that none of us wants to let the young girl I talked about earlier, to go hungry, to get abused, or to sleep in the cold night of December on the road, when our daughters and granddaughters are sleeping safe and sound – as they should.

Thank you.

NARENDRA MODI

2014

Speech at FICCI, Ahmedabad

The 15th and current Prime Minister of India, Narendra Damodardas Modi is a prominent leader of the Bhartiya Janta Party (BJP). Serving as the Chief Minister of Gujarat from 2001-2014, he is credited for creating a tremendous rate of economic growth in the state. A key strategist for BJP, he led the party to win the 2014 general election by outright majority in the Lok Sabha, attaining the coveted post of the Prime Minister of the country on May 16, 2014. An inspiring leader, Modi is a perfect example of hard-work and determined focus. Known to have worked as a tea-seller during his boyhood, he has come a long way, reaching the pinnacles of success, and still looking forward.

Showing praiseworthy enthusiasm since the beginning, he was given the charge of ABVP (the student wing of RSS) very early on in his career. He worked actively in the RSS and BJP in the following years. With steady confidence and intense optimism, he clearly expresses his views, not shying away from criticizing other Government parties for their ways. Although admired for his economic reforms, policies and growth in Gujarat, he has also been criticized for the dismal state of affairs of the Human Development Index in the state.

On January 15, 2014, then Prime Ministerial candidate for BJP, Narendra Modi addressed the first National Executive Committee meeting of FICCI (Federation of Indian Chambers of Commerce and Industry) in Gandhinagar, Ahmedabad. This meet was organized against the backdrop of slowdown of the Indian economy and prevailing unemployment. Through this speech, Modi presented his vision of a better India and the management of its economy, while sidelining the previous party for their 'mismanagement' of the Indian economy. He talked about the nation's overall development, the need to have an element of trust between the government, business and society and about industries and employment.

Speech at FICCI, Ahmedabad, 2014

I got an opportunity to come among you before. But there is difference between the situation back then and what it is now. Back then I came because if a program happens in Gujarat and the Chief Minister does not attend, it does not look or feel good. I have been invited now so that we can together decide upon the direction in which our country should go. So I believe that everything being said from this pedestal is important. And every word has its own meaning. There are lots of expectations. And the number of words Birla (ji) said in his each sentence, if we touch upon each word of it, we'll have to spend a week to understand them. If we let go of the small things, we should at least hold on to the bigger issue.

In the 21st century, there was this positivity in the country. It felt as if the country was full of energy in the direction of growth. In the middle of the twentieth century, there were talks of the arrival of the 21st century but it failed to inspire. It was as if a family was discussing where they would spend their vacations. Such was the talk about the 21st century's arrival as if it were Christmas vacation. And this is how we wasted the mid of the 20th century. Had we decided upon a direction, plan of implementation, distribution of work, had we worked upon the usage of resources back then, we would have given a better grounding and foundation to the country. But we lost the chance.

The first part of 21st century was full of confidence and courage. We may have differences on the statistical data but there was a faith generated that we as a nation can do something. We can move ahead. Unfortunately, everything lost its rigor. The air is full of doubt and insensitivity. It is important for us to come out of this situation. The way to come back is by regaining trust from all the social spheres except politics. For example, if a child goes to give an examination, and a teacher does not teach the syllabus again, rather encourages the child filling them with self confidence, the child passes with flying colours.

These things have an impact in all spheres of life, be it the player walking in the field, the hard work that a coach gives in for years, that is one thing and performance of the player in the field is another. It takes one positive result to reverse the direction of flow of faith in the nation. When there is disappointment in all directions and 7-8 nations together organize a world cup that we win, it raises the energy and confidence in us. All it takes is confidence to win the world cup. Why? The person who is immersed in depression he does not want to stay in the same plane. He wants to jump back out of it. All he needs is a ray of hope. If this is the biggest priority of our nation then who should we trust with it? I do not believe that one grand public address will make you believe in your capabilities or win in your trust. Nobody can do that.

Society takes note of every miniscule detail before deciding upon it. We have had a bad experience in the past that we are finding it tough to trust someone with our expectations. We need to trust carefully or else we'll be betrayed again. Therefore, it is important to have an air of trust around. I am saying that with experience in Gujrat.

Though I have not met all the investors in India, nor have had an opportunity to interact with all, I have managed to interact with 10-15% on one to one basis. And they all feel that they can head towards Gujarat, work freely. Independent of whether they have met me or not, they have worked with the government or not, whether they have seen our rules and regulations or not; they are aware of my policies, but somebody said that their experience has been great. And this trust changes the situation.

Now that I meet big corporate owners, I feel I have done my work properly and am over with my responsibility. I hope that nobody says that they came here just for the sake of it. When they leave they know that it wouldn't happen. When you walk in you still know it wouldn't happen - such is the lack of faith. This situation does not allow our nation to move ahead, friends. And, therefore, leadership plays an important role. Do you have the courage to take the decisions without moving? Do you have the courage to trust your instincts based on your experience? Do you have the courage to swim against the tide? Do you have the courage to bring out the sinking/ broken boat out of the river? The time demands us to stand up and answer these questions.

We set the agenda and inspire people. If the purchasing power of each individual goes down then what will happen? Have our economic policies and economy paid heed to such things so that the purchasing power of individual increases? Purchasing power will increase only with the increase in income. The income will increase with employment; they are not a part of the stages of production and growth. Mahatma Gandhi once said, "The gain by the one in the lowest strata of society determines the success of the policy." All I want to say is, we can increase the income of the person in the lowest strata of society.

Villagers are the biggest buyers, but their purchasing power is low. And the economy of the cities will not be generated. If the economy of the city does not generate itself, then all our corporate organizations and industry would be limited to banks. So, generation of economy in villages should be emphasized upon. We know that the two sectors with the biggest purchasing power are the agricultural sector and the service sector.

Masses of land cannot be increased in the agricultural sector. As a fact, the masses of land are reducing. The land size is reducing in a way. The size of a family increases; then they had five brothers and now have twenty-five in the second and third generation. The piece of land will be divided into as many pieces. In that situation, our focus should be on how to increase the productivity. Then will come the stage when productivity alone will not serve the matter. How to have value addition in that case? We do not complete this chain economically. Then we cannot change the economic condition of the villages.

So how should we attach the development of corporate industry with this so that our farmers get the opportunity of value addition? Ultimately value addition is the sum of industry and agriculture. The best combination, rather. In a country like ours, there is a need to emphasize on this. I believe that our policies should be worked upon that level. Industrial growth - there are controversies and debates around them in our country. There are many intellectuals who keep on trying to show the path to the country - day and night. But if you want employment, then you need to develop people. It has been accepted worldwide. But if leave our resources then we'll get neither employment nor industry. There is a need to have value addition to our raw natural resources. The value of our natural resources is almost the same as that of our agriculture. The value addition to water produces electricity.

Water is used in everyday chores and when added with value, leads to the production of electricity, which further helps in employing people. We should have a holistic vision towards all our natural resources. Be it the sector of wind energy, solar energy, hydro or steel manufacturing or conversion of stone to cement - in a country like ours the resources like bauxite are not utilized. Everything is wasted and underutilized. These can be used for the purpose of blowing samajwadi views in public. What kind of country is this where there are so many resources which can be stolen with the help of certain people while there is no value addition to them? Had there been any value addition, our economy would have been generated. We could have worked in the direction of uniform growth.

When we talk about growth, the issue of infrastructure crops in. When you talk about infrastructure, the sector of energy jumps in. Road is not limited by way. Development of roads does not mean working corporate. We need energy. The question is: what kind of country is this where industries worth 20000MW energy is shut? Why? Because we have no fuel. Why do we have no fuel? Because of policy paralysis. What should we do? Import coal. Import increases as a result, due to which the current deficit increases. Current account deficit increases, leading to lowering of money value. You see, wrong policy orientation shows its result individually on each and everything. Do you need a long term and big vision for this? Do you need any expert from various international firms? It is very easy to correct these things; all you need to take is responsibility. It shouldn't be like we are ready for garlands while running away from pelting stones.

This is the reason for disappointment. When the nation gives us a responsibility - we have to take it regardless of whether the responsibility is good or bad. A nation cannot survive if you are running away. And running is a fashion these days, I observe. People ask me why I did not run away from the Patna rally. There were bomb blasts and I was there. This is the responsibility of leadership. In Surat, during the floods we suffered major losses. Now you know that such a situation brings in the interested media. It's like a doctor refusing to leave the city in the month of September, for it being the season of business. People like these behave in a particular manner in this situation. Calamity is a like a season for journalists. Everything that I'll do or say will be a doomsday for them. In such a situation, any leader who visits them will have to bear the brunt of people's anger - they'll tear off your clothes.

I remember visiting Surat. I was there for 3 days and nights. I was cleaning things as late as 2 AM at night. One day the media attacked me. They fought but I did not run away. The same people who printed against me were my (pretentious) friends the very next day. This was our testing time. It is our responsibility to face it all with open arms and broad shoulders. I say, we have demographic division and I believe that the 21st century is the century for Asia with India and China leading. India has two powers of which one is its demographic division and the other being division of democracy. Ours is the biggest democracy in the world. It is a way to tell the world. We have the opportunity. Democracy attracts people. Our vibrant system, democracy and judicial system gives faith to the world to come in to us. Do we have trust on that faith? We live in times where 65% of our population is below the age of 35. We don't have any mission of skill development. As they say, we need people and are not able to find them. There is only one way to accomplish this: skill development. We took help of the technology. Industrialists were afraid of apprenticeship law, afraid that they will have to employ them later. This was the general outlook.

In Gujarat, we collected people with small and big businesses. We taught them that the law is not like this. Take this in spirit, as spirit. And they gained faith and courage to give opportunity to the youngsters. When we tried it at first, we asked them of their requirements. We made a portal listing out the industry and asking the younger lot to choose the industry they wish to go to. We built an online mechanism. And we managed to generate employment for one lakh people. When we realized that it's a good experimentation, we started letting out 1500 rupees from the government fund. As a result, the industrialists who had kept 10 apprentices could utilize 2 out of them. He started receiving quality manpower. Earlier he had shut down his industry out of fear. He used to think that he'll be trapped. But on explanation, he realized that he'll not face any such problem.

How should we develop these situations and enhance skill development? The way our government syllabus works is old-school. The way automobiles used to work in 1960s is taught in our institutes. The advanced ways and technological development go past the students as they have not been taught the advances. It should be dynamic in nature and not rigid. And we have a solution. We told the industrial houses that these are ITI and you need a particular kind of trained manpower. So you start your own syllabus in these institutions. You recruit 50 of these - teach them and take them with your industry. We developed this PPP model with the help of which we efficiently - without wasting money, time and human resources - developed the best manpower. If we think we can, we can.

And now we see that despite being an engineer there are many companies which say that though he/she is educated but can't work the way we want them to. So we started online education. If they are in there fourth year of engineering, we asked them to go to Microsoft to find the syllabus. Satellite system which has been developed to teach will be charged Rs. 100. So the course, for which you earlier had to pay Rs. 25000 if you go to the market, was available at the cost of Rs. 100. That youngster when passes out from college immediately joins Microsoft. So we have to develop the manpower which is needed by the country in next five to ten years. You'd know when Gujarat promotes a vibrant Gujarat model, one angle which never finds space in media, is that those who do MOU, later have a round table conference here, after a week, 15 days and/or month. In that conference, there is government, university and investor.

We ask the investor - if you are going to do this particular thing, you'd need land, infrastructure etc, but what kind of manpower do you need? How many people, with what capabilities and skills? According to that we ask our universities to update their syllabus. Here, he develops his factory and simultaneously manpower is developed. If we do not develop according to an integrated and holistic approach, where there is industry, it will lack manpower, where there is industry there is no material, even if we have industry and raw material - we don't have energy. Where there is energy, factory and raw material on the day of inaugural, the officer is missing. The vehicle is at one place. These small lapses are not because of lack of vision but because of lack of commitment. Due to this, such conditions are generated. If someone takes the responsibility to rectify these miniscule details, the results will reflect.

In our country these days, the PM uses a word regularly - inclusive growth. He likes it, so he says it. But if we don't make weaker families strong and sufficient enough, don't built in capacity - through education - we cannot make them sufficient, we won't be able to turn around the situation. We have to include them in the process of development. If there is development somewhere - it shouldn't be like if you stand in the queue you'll find your way in. If there is a new temple being built somewhere - you stand in there and you'll manage. We have to make them self sufficient. Ultimately that will show in the final outcome, through skill development and education.

Again and again he popularizes this inclusive growth and he feels good, but if we do not make a poor family sufficient, not building capacity, we will not be able to make him capable and hence, not be able to change the circumstances.

We have to make them partners in the mechanism of growth, through the medium of skill development, through the medium of education, by way of installing small-small industries, giving strength to the service sector. I am surprised at how we chant tourism-tourism-tourism, the business worth three trillion and how the world sees every village, every alley. Our every stone talks, but we do not give emphasis on this. Some people came to meet me recently and I talked about it in TV channels: Indian idol programmes, among singers, dancers, performances of children. I asked them to have competitions for people as to who performs as the best guide. We will give out prizes. He might, for instance, show that in his own village there is Modhera's Sun temple; he will come with it and put it on the screen and provide details. You judge the tracing, style of talking and give him feedback. You will see lakhs of youths evolving out as guides as a profession. Two aims would be accomplished: with TV, people will watch advertisements in villages and also would appreciate the importance of tourism and guides. We will also promote the service sector. Example, in the health sector today, the world still looks for the cheapest best health facilities and people get the confidence that they have no problem after visiting a doctor. Today, doctors and hospitals are counted, but the subject of insurance has struck as such no one. If the people of world get to know that we get our treatment in India then there is probability of insurance in India. So the cost of getting a tooth extraction is much cheaper here than in their country and we also feel proud that we should extract the teeth of someone.

Focus should be also given these things as we focus on many other things in the direction of development in these days: there is a storm relating to current deficit in the Government. Four different people say four different things. This is very amazing but you tell me, in a very short time in the coming days our import of electronic goods will exceed the import of petroleum products. I am talking about the experience of the industry sector. If you focus on profits and profits, and if the thought of making world class products did not occur to you, there's no point. The reason behind such a big import in the country is that we cannot build these products. Therefore, I think that things should be decided by sitting with the industrialists. You have made such profits, now make 20 percent in it and we have no objections, but to save the country you will make some contribution. If someone tells him, for instance, the country needs salt and the production of salt is very small, profit is very low, and the country needs it and we call 25 industrialists of the country and say to them, "You make profits, but this time give emphasis on salt. We cannot let the country stay without salt." You tell me if he will do it or not.

In our country there is lack of power of the youth. We should encourage them. Some changes are required. For example, the railways. There is a huge business in railway, the manpower required by that railway, who can come from anywhere by doing DA, degree, diploma, and they take them. Should the railway have its own four universities? It is not necessary to built something new. Four existing universities could be dedicated for the railway cause. These universities should be converted for the trade of railways. Thus would generate the skilled manpower required by the railway. If the efficiency of railway will increase, it will act as a major force to generate the economy of India. It's possible. In our country there is a huge shortfall of officers. How will the business run? Why can't we have a university of defence and then the promising youths of the country could go there and study and after that, fill the posts of officers lying vacant in defence. The security in the country will stand in unique form.

The sum of the talk is that friends all these things are possible. And if we want we can change the situations and I said earlier that I am very optimistic. I have no negativity. If I show someone a glass having half-water, some would say half is full and some would say half is empty. I have a third mind-set. I would say it is half-filled with water, half-filled with air, so the glass is all full. This is the subject of thinking. I feel good about being here amongst you. My best wishes to you that you come to such a land in whose blood there is money, entrepreneurship, courage, and power. You also take some of that power and come forward to change the destiny of the country.

Many-many wishes, thanks.

NARENDRA MODI

2014

Independence Day Speech

Narendra Modi is the 15th and current Prime Minister of India, attaining the coveted post of the PM by way of a historical win in the 16th Lok Sabha Elections in May, 2014. Narendra Modi has since then taken the country and the world by the storm. Be it creating a buzz wherever he speaks, or his ideas to take the country forward, Modi has attracted indefinite attention from all over the world.

Among the first fine displays of his strong oratory skills, this Independence Day Speech delivered from Red Fort on August 15, 2014, managed to capture the attention of the nation. In this hour-long extempore speech, Prime Minister Narendra Modi mentioned and extended his thanks to every Indian hero, leader, government and person, with whose efforts the country stands today where it does. He addressed the citizens of the country, motivating them to follow the path of brotherhood and shun all evils responsible for dividing the society. Narendra Modi, in this speech, touched upon many ideas and practices close to the hearts of Indians. Among the most popular is the announcement of the Clean India Campaign, where he propagates cleanliness as one of the most important tasks every citizen must undertake. The Digital

India Campaign was also announced in this speech.

By way of his inspiring words, relevant examples and quoting influential leaders, Modi managed to have a strong impact on everyone, especially the youth. His ideas come with full-fledged plans and achievable objectives. They mostly provide definite solutions, which makes it all the more influential. This speech signifies the ideas of a leader who took over the responsibility of a country that desperately needs good leadership.

Independence Day Speech, 2014

My dear countrymen,

Today, all Indians in the country and abroad are celebrating the festival of independence. On this sacred festival of independence, the prime servant of India extends greetings to all dear countrymen.

I am present amidst you not as the Prime Minister, but as the Prime Servant. The freedom struggle was fought for so many years, so many generations laid down their lives, innumerable people sacrificed their lives and youth, spent their entire lives behind bars. Today, I pay my respect, greetings and homage to all those who laid their lives for the country's independence.

I also pay my respects to the crores of citizens of this country on the pious occasion of India's independence, and recall all those martyrs who laid down their lives in India's struggle for freedom. The day of independence is a festival when we take a solemn pledge of working for the welfare of Mother India, and also for the welfare of the poor, oppressed, Dalits, the exploited and the backward people of our country.

My dear countrymen, a national festival is an occasion to refine and rebuild the national character. This national festival inspires us to resolve ourselves to lead a life where our character gets refined further, to dedicate ourselves to the nation, and have our every activity linked to the interest of the nation. Only then this festival of freedom can be a festival of inspiration to take India to newer heights.

My dear countrymen, this nation has neither been built by political leaders nor by rulers nor by governments. This nation has been built by our farmers, our workers, our mothers and sisters, our youth. The country has reached here today because of the generation to generation rigours undertaken by our sages, our saints, our maestros, our teachers, our scientists and social workers. These great people and these great generations who had worked for the country throughout their lives, deserve our deepest respect.

This is the beauty of India's Constitution, this is its capability which has made it possible that today a boy from a small town, a poor family, has got the opportunity to pay homage to the tricolour of India at the ramparts of Lal Quila (Red Fort). This is the strength of India's democracy. This is an invaluable legacy which we have inherited from the architects of our Constitution. I pay my respects to those architects of the Constitution of India today.

Brothers and sisters, today if we have reached here after independence, it is because of the contribution of all the Prime Ministers, all the governments and even the governments of all the states. I want to express my feelings of respect and gratitude to all those previous governments and ex-Prime Ministers who have endeavoured to take our present day India to such heights and who have added to the country's glory.

This country has been built on such foundations of

ancient cultural heritage, where we were told only one mantra during Vedic period, which is indicative of our work culture and that we have learned - *"Sangachchhdhvam samvadadhvam sam wo manansi jaanataam."* We walk together, we move together, we think together, we resolve together and together we take this country forward.

Having imbibed this basic mantra, 125 crore countrymen have taken the nation forward. Yesterday only the first parliamentary session of the new government had concluded.

Today, I can proudly say that the session of Parliament reflects our thinking and it is a reflection of our intentions. We are not for moving forward on the basis or virtue of majority. We want to move ahead on the basis of strong consensus - *"Sangachhadhwam"* and therefore, the nation has witnessed the entire session of Parliament.

Having taken all the parties and opposition along while working shoulder to shoulder, we achieved an unprecedented success and the credit for this does not go to the Prime Minister alone, the credit does not go to the people sitting in the government, the credit for this goes to the opposition also, the credit goes to all the leaders and members of the opposition.

From the ramparts of Red Fort, quite proudly I salute all the Members of Parliament, I also salute all the political parties and by virtue of their strong support, we could take some important decisions intended to take the nation forward.

Brothers and sisters, I am an outsider for Delhi; I am not a native of Delhi. I have no idea about the administration and working of this place. I have been quite isolated from the elite class of this place but during the last two months while being an outsider, I had an insider view and I was astonished. It is not a political platform, rather it is a platform of a national policy and, therefore, my views should not be evaluated from a political perspective.

I have already said, I salute all the ex-Prime Ministers and earlier governments who have brought the country thus far. But I am going to say something else and it may not be seen from a political point of view. When I came to Delhi and looked at things from an insider view, I felt what it was and I was surprised to see it. It seemed as if dozens of separate governments are running at the same time in one main government. It appeared that everyone has their own fiefdom. I could observe disunity and conflict among them. One department is taking on the other department and taking on to the extent that two departments of the same government are fighting against each other by approaching Supreme Court. This disunity, this conflict among people of the same country! How can we take the country forward? That is why I have started making efforts to raze those walls; I have started making efforts at making the government not an assembled entity, but an organic unity, an organic entity, a harmonious whole - with one aim, one mind, one direction, one energy.

Let's resolve to steer the country to one destination. We have it in us to move in that direction. A few days back... Nowadays newspapers are full of news that Modi-ji's government has come, officers are reaching office on time, offices open in time, and people get there in time. I observed that India's national newspapers, TV media were carrying these news items prominently.

As the head of government I could have derived pleasure in the fact that everything started going on time, cleanliness got the attention it deserved, but I was not taking pleasure, I was feeling pained. Why? Because if government officers arrive office in time, does that make news? And if that makes news, it shows how low we have fallen. It is proof of that, and is that how, brothers and sisters, the governments have run? Today in the face of global competition, when we have to realise the dreams of millions of Indians, the country cannot run on the lines of "it happens", "it goes".

In order to fulfill the aspirations of masses, we have to sharpen the tool called 'government machinery', we have to make it keen, more dynamic, and it is in this direction that we are working.

My countrymen, it's not long since I have come from outside Delhi, but I give you an assurance that the people in the government are very capable - from the peon to the Cabinet Secretary, everybody is capable, everybody has a power, they have experience. I want to awaken that power, I want to unite that power and want to accelerate the pace of the welfare of nation through that power and I shall definitely do it. I want to assure the countrymen that we will achieve that, we will definitely do that. I could not say this on 16th May, but today after my experience of two-two and half months, keeping the Tricolour as witness, I am saying on 15th of August that it is possible, and it will be achieved.

Brothers and sisters, the time has come to give serious

thought to the fact, whether we have a duty to create India of the dreams of those great people who gave us freedom, or do we have a national character? Can someone please tell me if anyone has ever introspected in the evening after a full day's work as to whether his or her acts have helped the poor of the country or not, whether his or her actions have resulted in safeguarding the interest of the country or not, whether the actions have been directed in the country's welfare or not? Should it not be the motto of one and a quarter billion countrymen that every step in life should be in the country's interests?

Unfortunately, we have an environment today wherein if you approach anyone with some work, he begins by saying, "What does it mean for me?" He begins by saying, "What does it have for me?" and when he comes to know that it does not entail any benefit for him, immediately he says, "Why should I bother?" We have to rise above these feelings. Everything is not for self-interest only. There are certain things which are meant for the country and we have to refine this national character. We have to rise above the feelings of "Why should I bother?" and "What does it mean for me?" and instead we have to think, "I am for the nation's interest and in this field, I am going to lead". We have to inculcate this sentiment.

Brothers and sisters, when we hear about the incidents of rape, we hang our heads in shame. People come out with different arguments, someone indulges in psycho analysis, but today from this platform, I want to ask those parents, I want to ask every parent, you have a daughter of 10 or 12 years' age, you are always on the alert, every now and then you keep on asking - where are you going, when would you come back, inform immediately after you reach. Parents ask their daughters hundreds of questions, but have any parents ever dared to ask their son as to where he is going, why he is going out, who his friends are? After all, a rapist is also somebody's son. He also has parents. As parents, have we ever asked our son as to what he is doing and where he is going? Try to do this with your sons as you do with your daughters. Can every parent decide to impose as many restrictions on the sons as have been imposed on our daughters?

My dear brothers and sisters, the law will take its own course, strict action will be taken, but as a member of the society, as parents, we also have some responsibilities.

If somebody tells me that those who have taken guns on their shoulders and killed innocent people are Maoists, terrorists, but they are also somebody's children, I would like to ask of such parents if they had ever asked their children as to why they were taking a wrong path. Every parent must take this responsibility; he must know that his misguided son is bent on killing innocent people. He is not able to serve himself or his family or the country. I want to say to those youngsters who have chosen the path of violence that whatever they are and wherever they are, it is all because of Mother India only that they have got it.

Whoever you are, it is all because of your parents. I want to ask you to think how green, how beautiful and how beneficial this earth can become if you shoulder the plough instead of the gun which spills blood on this land. How long shall we have bloodshed on this land, how long shall we take the lives of the innocent people and what have we got after all this? The path of violence has not yielded anything to us.

Brothers and sisters, I had gone to Nepal recently. There I said something publicly to draw the attention of the whole world. There was a time when the Emperor Ashoka who had chosen the path of wars, got converted to the path of Buddha at the sight of violence.

There was a time in Nepal when their youngsters had opted for the path of violence but today I witness that the same youngsters are waiting for their constitution. The same people associated with them are framing the constitution. If Nepal could present the best example of moving from the weapons to books, then it could provide inspiration to the youngsters in the world to abandon the path of violence.

Brothers and sisters, if Nepal, the land of Buddha, can give that message to the world, then why can't India do the same? So it's the call of the hour that we renounce the path of violence and take the path of brotherhood.

For one reason or the other, we have had communal tensions for ages. This led to the division of the country. Even after independence, we have had to face the poison of casteism and communalism. How long will these evils continue? Whom does it benefit? We have had enough of fights, many have been killed. Friends, look behind and you will find that nobody has benefited from it. Except casting a slur on Mother India, we have done nothing. Therefore, I appeal to all people, whether it is the poison of casteism, communalism, regionalism, discrimination on social and economic basis, all these are obstacles in our way forward. Let's resolve for once in our hearts; let's put a moratorium on all such activities for 10 years, we shall march ahead to a society which will be free from all such tensions. And you will see that how much strength we get from peace, unity, goodwill and brotherhood. Let`s experiment it for once.

My dear countrymen, believe in my words, I do assure you. Shun all the sins committed so far, give up that way, follow the way of goodwill and brotherhood, and let's resolve to take the country forward. I believe we can do that.

With advancement of science, brothers and sisters, we have a rising feeling of modernity in our mind, but what do we do? Have we ever thought what the sex ratio in the country is like? 940 girls are born against per 1,000 boys. Who is causing this imbalance in the society? Certainly not God. I request the doctors not to kill the girl growing in the womb of a mother just to line their own pockets. I advise mothers and sisters not to sacrifice daughters in the hope of a son. Sometimes parents feel tempted to have a son in the hope of having support in old age. I am a person who has worked in public life. I have come across families with five sons, each having bungalows, access to fleet of cars, but the parents are forced to live in old-age homes. I have seen such families. I have also seen families with only a daughter as progeny. That daughter sacrifices her dreams, doesn't get married, and spends her entire life in taking care of old parents.

This disparity points to female feticide and to the polluted and tainted minds the people in the 21st century have. We will have to liberate ourselves from it, and that is the message to us on this festival.

Recently Commonwealth Games were organised. Indian sportspersons brought glory to the country. Nearly 64 of our sportspersons won. They brought home 64 medals. Of them, 29 are girls. Let's feel proud and clap for them. Girls also contribute to India's fame and glory. Let's recognise it. Let's take them along, shoulder to shoulder. This way we can get over the evils that have crept in social life. Therefore, brothers and sisters, we have to proceed in that direction as a social and national character.

Brothers and sisters, development is the only way forward for the country. Good governance is the only way. There are only these two tracks to take the country forward - good governance and development, we can move forward only by taking them with us. We wish to move forward with the intent of taking them with us. When I ask a person what he does, if he in a private job, he says that he has a job; when you ask the same from a person in government, he says that he is in service. Both earn, but for one it is a 'job' while for the other it is 'service'. I ask a question from all brothers and sisters in government service, whether the word "service" has not lost its strength, its identity? People in government service are not doing a "job", they are doing "service". We have to revive this feeling, we have to take this feeling forward as a national character; we have to move forward in this direction.

Brothers and sisters, should the citizens of the country take steps for the welfare of the nation or not? Imagine, if these 125 crore countrymen move one step forward, then the country moves 125 crore steps forward. The meaning of democracy is not just limited to electing a government, but its meaning is that 125 crore of citizens work together, joining shoulders with the government to fulfill hopes and aspirations of the country. This is the meaning of democracy.

We have to create partnership with the people. We have to proceed under Public-Private Partnership. We have to proceed along with the participation of the people. But please tell me why our farmers commit suicide? A farmer takes loan from the moneylender, but fails to repay his loans. He takes loans for the wedding of his daughter, but fails to repay. He will have to suffer hardships during his whole life. He chooses to commit suicide. Who will save the poor families of such farmers?

I have come here with a pledge to launch a scheme on this festival of freedom. It will be called Pradhanmantri Jan-Dhan Yojana. I wish to connect the poorest citizens of the country with the facility of bank accounts through this *yojana*. There are millions of families who have mobile phones but no bank accounts. We have to change this scenario. Economic resources of the country should be utilized for the well-being of the poor. The change will commence from this point. This *yojana* will open the window. Therefore, an account holder under Pradhanmantri Jan-Dhan Yojana will be given a debit card. An insurance of Rs.1 lakh will be guaranteed with that debit card for each poor family, so that such families are covered with the insurance of Rs 1 lakh in case of any crisis in their lives.

My brothers and sisters, it is a country of young people. The 65 percent population of the country happens to be under the age of 35 years. Our country has the largest number of young in the world. Have we ever thought of deriving an advantage out of it? Today, the world needs skilled workforce. Today, India also needs skilled workforce. At times, we look for a good driver but he is not available, we look for a plumber, but he is not available. If we need a good cook, he is not available. We have young people, they are unemployed, but the kind of young people we seek are not available. If we have to promote the development of our country, then our mission has to be "skill development" and "skilled India".

Millions and millions of Indian youth should go for acquisition of skills and there should be a network across the country for this and not the archaic systems. They should acquire the skills which could contribute towards making India a modern country. Whenever they go to any country in the world, their skills must be appreciated, and we want to go for a two-pronged development.

I also want to create a pool of young people who are able to create jobs, and the ones who are not capable of creating jobs and do not have the opportunities, they must be in a position to face their counterparts in any corner of the world, while keeping their heads high by virtue of their hard work and their dexterity of hands, and win the hearts of people around the world through their skills. We want to go for capacity building of such young people. My brothers and sisters, having taken a resolve to enhance the skill development at a highly rapid pace, I want to accomplish this.

The world has undergone a change. My dear countrymen, the world has changed. Now India cannot decide its future by remaining isolated and sitting alone in a corner. The economics of the world have changed and, therefore, we will have to act accordingly. The government has taken many decisions recently, made some announcements in the budget and I call upon the world and call upon Indians spread over the world that if we have to provide more and more employment to the youth, we will have to promote the manufacturing sector. If we have to develop a balance between imports and exports, we will have to strengthen manufacturing sector. If we have to put in use the education, the capability of the youth, we will have to go for manufacturing sector and for this, Hindustan will have to lend its full strength, but we also invite world powers.

Therefore I want to appeal to all the people, world over, from the ramparts of Red Fort, "Come, Make in India", "Come, manufacture in India". Sell in any country of the world but manufacture here. We have got skill, talent, discipline, and determination to do something. We want to give the world a favourable opportunity to come here. "Come, Make in India" and we will say to the world, from electrical to electronics, "Come, Make in India", from automobiles to agro value addition, "Come, Make in India", paper or plastic, "Come, Make in India", satellite or submarine, "Come, Make in India". Our country is powerful. Come, I am giving you an invitation.

I want to call upon the youth of the country, particularly the small people engaged in the industrial sector. I want to call upon the youth working in the field of technical education in the country. As I say to the world, "Come, Make in India", I say to the youth of the country - it should be our dream that this message reaches every corner of the world. "Made in India", this should be our dream. In order to serve the country, is it necessary for the youth of the country to be hanged like Bhagat Singh? Brothers and sisters, Lal Bahadur Shastri had given the slogan, "Jai Jawan, Jai Kisan". A soldier sacrifices himself at the border and protects Mother India. Similarly, a farmer serves Mother India by filling godowns with grains. This is also nation's service. Filling the granary is the biggest nation's service that a farmer provides.

Brothers and Sisters, I would like to pose a question to my youngsters as to why despite them, we are forced to import even the smallest of things? My country's youth can resolve it, they should conduct research, try to find out what type of items are imported by India and then each one should resolve that, through micro or small industries perhaps, he would manufacture at least one such item, so that we need not import the same in future. We should even advance to a situation wherein we are able to export such items. If each one of our millions of youngsters resolves to manufacture at least one such item, India can become a net exporter of goods. I, therefore, urge upon the youth, in particular our small entrepreneurs that they would never compromise, at least on two counts. First, zero defect and, second, zero effect. We should manufacture goods in such a way that they carry zero defect, that our exported goods are never returned to us. We should manufacture goods with zero effect that they should not have a negative impact on the environment. If we march ahead with the dream of zero defect in the manufacturing sector, then, my brothers and sisters, I am confident that we would be able to achieve our goals.

The youth of India has completely transformed the identity of India in the world. Earlier, in what manner did the world know our country? Till only 25-30 years back, if not more, there were many people in the world who thought that

India was a country of snake charmers, it was a country which practiced black magic.

The real identity of India had not reached the world, but my dear brothers and sisters, our youngsters, 20-22-23 years old youngsters have mesmerized the whole world with their skills in computers. Our young IT professionals have provided a new path of making a new identity of India. If our country has this strength, can we think of something about the country? Our dream is, therefore, of "Digital India". When I talk of "Digital India", I don't speak of the elite, it is for the poor people.

You can imagine what quality education the children in villages will get if all the villages of India are connected with broadband connectivity and if we are able to give long-distance education to the schools in every remote corner of the villages. If we create a network of telemedicine in places where there is a shortage of doctors, we can have clear guidelines of the way in which health facilities have to be provided to the poor people living in those areas.

The citizens of India have mobile phones in their hands, they have mobile connectivity, but can we walk in the direction of mobile governance? We have to move in a direction where every poor person is able to operate his bank account from his mobile, is able to demand various things from the government, can submit applications, can conduct all his business, while on the move, through mobile governance and if this has to be done, we have to move towards 'Digital India, and if we have to move towards Digital India, then we have a dream.

Today we are importing electronic goods on a large scale. Friends, you will be surprised that we are bringing in these televisions, mobile phones, iPads and all these electronic goods. It is a necessity to import petroleum products, oil, diesel and petrol. Second to this is the import of our electronic goods. If we move ahead with the dream of Digital India to manufacture electronic goods and become self-reliant at least there, how big can the benefit for the treasury be! Therefore, e-governance is what we need to take this idea of Digital India forward.

E-governance is easy governance, effective governance and also economic governance. E-governance paves the way for good governance. There was a time when we used to say that railways provided connectivity to the country. That was it. I say that today it is IT that has the potential to connect each and every citizen of the country and that is why we want to realise the mantra of unity with the help of Digital India.

Brothers and sisters, if we move ahead with all this, then I believe that a Digital India will have the potential to stand with the world on equal footing. Our youth have that capability; it is an opportunity for them.

We want to promote tourism. Tourism provides employment to the poorest of the poor. A gram seller earns something, auto-rickshaw driver earns something, *pakoda* seller earns something and tea-seller also earns something. When there is talk of tea-seller, I feel a sense of belongingness. Tourism provides employment to the poorest of the poor. But there is a big obstacle in promoting tourism and in our national character, and that is - the filthiness all around us. Whether after independence, after so many years of independence, when we stand at the threshold of one and half decade of 21st century, we still want to live in filthiness? The first work I started here after formation of government is of cleanliness. People wondered whether it is a work of a Prime Minister. People may feel that it is a trivial work for a Prime Minister, but for me this big work. Cleanliness is very big work. Can't our country be clean? If 125 crore countrymen decide that they will never spread filthiness, which power in the world has the ability to spread filthiness in our cities and villages? Can't we resolve this much?

Brothers and sisters, it will be the 150th birth anniversary of Mahatma Gandhi in 2019. How do we celebrate 150th birth anniversary of Mahatma Gandhi? Mahatma Gandhi, who gave us freedom, who brought so much honour to such a big country in the world, what do we give to Mahatma Gandhi? He had cleanliness and sanitation closest to his heart. We resolve not to leave a speck of dirt in our village, city, street, area, school, temple, hospital by 2019 when we celebrate the 150th anniversary of Mahatma Gandhi. This happens not just with the government, but with public participation. That's why we have to do it together.

Brother and Sisters, we are living in 21st century. Has it ever pained us that our mothers and sisters have to defecate in open? Is not the dignity of women our collective responsibility? The poor womenfolk of the village wait for the night; until darkness descends, they can't go out to defecate. What bodily torture they must be feeling, how many diseases might that act engender. Can't we just make arrangements for toilets for the dignity of our mothers and sisters?

Brothers and Sisters, somebody might feel that a big festival like 15th August is an occasion to talk big. Talking big has its importance, making announcements too has importance, but sometimes announcements raise hopes and when the hopes are not fulfilled, the society sinks into a state of despondency. That's why we are in favour of telling those things which we can fulfill just within our sight. You must be getting shocked to hear the Prime Minister speaking of cleanliness and the need to build toilets from the ramparts of the Red Fort.

I do not know how my speech is going to be criticised and how will people take it. But this is my heartfelt conviction. I come from a poor family, I have seen poverty. The poor need respect and it begins with cleanliness. I, therefore, have to launch a "Clean India" campaign from 2nd October this year and carry it forward in four years. I want to make a beginning today itself and that is - all schools in the country should have toilets with separate toilets for girls. Only then our daughters will not be compelled to leave schools midway. Our parliamentarians utilising MPLAD funds are there. I appeal to them to spend it for constructing toilets in schools for a year. The government should utilise its budget on providing toilets. I call upon the corporate sector also to give priority to the provision of toilets in schools with your expenditure under Corporate Social Responsibility. This target should be finished within one year with the help of state governments and on the next 15th August, we should be in a firm position to announce that there is no school in India without separate toilets for boys and girls.

Brothers and sisters, if we proceed with the dreams, we

are in a position to realise them. Today, I wish to tell one more specific thing. It has its own importance to discuss matters and express the views of nation's interest. However, our Members of Parliament do not get an opportunity, though they are willing to do something. They can express themselves, write to the government, agitate, give memoranda. Still they do not get the opportunity to do something on their own.

Today I have come to you with a new idea. We are running so many schemes in the name of the Prime Minister in our country. There are numerous schemes in the name of various leaders. However, today I am going to announce a scheme on behalf of the Member of Parliament - Sansad Aadarsh Gram Yojana. We shall fix some parameters. I urge upon the Members of Parliament to select any one of the villages having population of three to five thousand in your constituency. The parameters will be according to the time, space and situation of that locality. It will include the conditions of health, cleanliness, atmosphere, greenery, cordiality etc.

On the basis of those parameters, each of our MPs should make one village of his or her constituency a Model Village by 2016. Can't we do at least this? Shouldn't we do this? If we have to build a nation, we should start from the village. Make a Model Village. The reason of fixing this target for 2016 is that it is a new scheme. It takes time to formulate a scheme and then to implement it. After 2016, select two more villages for this purpose, before we go for the General Elections in 2019. And after 2019, each Member of Parliament, during his/her tenure of five years must establish at least five model villages in his/her area. I also call upon the Members of Parliament from urban areas to adopt one village of their choice.

I also urge upon the Members of Parliament from Rajya Sabha to adopt one of the villages. If we provide one model village in each district of India, then the surrounding villages shall be automatically inspired to follow that model. Let us establish a model village, let us establish a village well-equipped with all systems and facilities. The birth anniversary of Jai Prakash Narayan Ji happens to be on 11th October.

On 11th October, the occasion of the birth anniversary of Jai Prakash Narayan Ji, I will present a complete blueprint of Sansad Adarsh Gram Yojana (Members of Parliament Model Village Scheme) before all Members of Parliament and State Governments, and I urge upon State Governments also that as per the feasibility in their respective states, all the Members of Legislative Assembly resolve to establish a model village. You can imagine all the Members of Legislative Assembly and all the Members of Parliament in the country establishing a model village. All of a sudden, there would be a model village in each block of India which could inspire us to transform the amenities in rural areas and could give us a new direction and, therefore, we want to move ahead under this Sansad Adarsh Gram Yojana.

Ever since our government has taken charge, there has been a discussion in the newspapers, on TV channels as to what would happen to Planning Commission. I believe that when Planning Commission was constituted, it was done on the basis of the circumstances and the needs of those times. In recent years, Planning Commission has contributed to the growth of the country in its own way. I respect that, I am proud of that, but the prevalent situation in the country is different, the global scenario has also changed, governments are no longer the centre of economic activities, the scope of such activities has broadened. State governments have been at the center of development and I consider this a good indication. If we have to take India forward, it can happen only by taking the states forward.

India's federal structure is more important today than in the last 60 years. To strengthen our federal structure, to make our federal structure vibrant, to take our federal structure a heritage of development, a team of Chief Ministers and Prime Minister should be there, a joint team of the Centre and the states should move forward. Then to do this job, we will have to think about giving the Planning Commission a look. So, I am saying from the rampart of the Red Fort that it is a very old system and it will have to be rejuvenated, it will have to be changed a lot. Sometimes it costs more to repair the old house, but it gives us no satisfaction. Thereafter, we have a feeling that it would be better to construct a new house altogether and therefore within a short period, we will replace the Planning Commission with a new institution having a new design and structure, a new body, a new soul, a new thinking, a new direction, a new faith towards forging a new direction to lead the country, based on creative thinking, public-private partnership, optimum utilization of resources, utilization of youth-power of the nation, to promote the aspirations of state governments seeking development, to empower the state governments and to empower the federal structure. Very shortly, we are about to move in a direction when this institute would be functioning in place of Planning Commission.

Brothers and sisters, today, on 15th August, we also have the birth anniversary of Maharishi Aurobindo. Maharishi

Aurobindo, being a rebel, moved on to achieve the status of a Yoga Guru. With regard to the destiny of India, he remarked, "I have a faith that the divine power and spiritual heritage of India will play an important role towards the welfare of the world." Such sentiments were echoed by Maharishi Arvind. I strongly believe in the words of legends. I have great faith in the statements made by ascetics, sages and saints and that's why today at the ramparts of Lal Quila I am reminded of the words of Swami Viveknanda. He had said - "I can see before my eyes Mother India awakening once again. My Mother India would be seated as the World Guru. Every Indian would render service towards welfare of humanity. This legacy of India would be useful for the welfare of the world". These words were spoken by Swami Viveknanda ji in his own style. Friends, the words of Viveknanda ji can never be untrue. He had a dream of seeing India ensconced as World Guru, his vision. It is incumbent upon us to realize that dream. This capable country, blessed with natural bounty, this country of youth, can do much for the world in the coming days.

Brothers and sisters, our foreign policy is a much talked-about issue. I clearly believe that India's foreign policy can be multi-dimensional. But there is an important issue to which I want to draw your attention. The way we fought for freedom, we fought together; we were not separate at that time. We were together. Which was the government with us? What were the weapons available to us? There was a Gandhi, a Sardar and lakhs of freedom fighters and such a huge empire. Didn't we win in the struggle of freedom against that empire? Did we not defeat the foreign powers? Did we not force them to leave India? We were the ones; they were our ancestors only who showed this might. If the people of India could remove such a big empire without the power of the government, without weapons and even without resources, then friends, it is the need of the hour to eradicate poverty, can we not overcome poverty? Can we not defeat poverty? My 125 crore dear countrymen, let us resolve to eradicate poverty, to win against it. Let us move with the dream of poverty eradication from India. Our neighbouring countries are also faced with the same problem. Why not get together with all the SAARC nations to plan out the fight against poverty? Let's fight together and defeat poverty. Let us see at least for once, how wonderful is the feeling of being alive instead of killing and getting killed.

This is the land where incidents from Siddharth's life happened. One bird was shot with an arrow by one brother and the other took out that arrow to save it. They went to their mother - whose bird, whose swan? Whether killer's or saviour's? The mother replied, 'saviour's'. The saviour has more power than the killer and that made him Buddha in the future. And that's why I seek cooperation from neighbouring countries for fighting against poverty in concert and cooperate with them, so that together with SAARC countries we can create our importance and emerge as a power in the world. It is imperative that we work together with a dream to win a fight against poverty, shoulder to shoulder.

I went to Bhutan, Nepal; all the dignitaries from SAARC countries took part in oath-taking ceremony. This marked a good beginning. This will definitely yield good results, it is my belief and this thinking of India, in the country and the world, that we want to do well to the countrymen and be useful for the welfare of the world, India wants such a hand to be extended. We are trying to move forward with these dreams to achieve them.

Brothers and sisters, today on 15th August, we will resolve to do something for the country. Let's be useful for the country, we will move ahead with a resolve to take the country forward, and I assure you, brothers and sisters, as well as my colleagues in the Government, that if you work for 12 hours, I will do so for 13 hours. If you work for 14 hours, I will do for 15 hours. Why? Because I'm among you not as a Prime Minister, but as the first servant. I have formed the government not as a ruler, but as a servant.

Brothers and sisters, I assure that this country has a destiny. It is destined to work for the welfare of the world. It was said by Vivekanand ji. India is born; this Hindustan is born in order to achieve this destiny. 125 crore countrymen have to move forward wholeheartedly for the welfare of the nation.

Once again I feel proud of the devotion, the sacrifices of the security forces of the country, para-military forces of the country, all the security forces of the country, to protect Mother India. I say to the countrymen, 'Eternal vigilance is the price of liberty'.

The army is vigilant. We should also be vigilant as the country scales new heights. We have to move forward with this resolution. Speak loudly with me with full force - *Bharat Mata ki jai! Jai Hind! Vande Mataram!*

SOURCES

Efforts have been made to utilize the most authentic sources and permissions for all speeches included in this book. For some of them however, we had to make do with the best and most suitable, available source. In case you recognize yourself to hold the right to any speech, please be in touch with us.

References -

1. J.R.D. Tata, Letters, Rupa & Co. (2004)

2. http://www.gandhi-manibhavan.org/gandhicomesalive/speech3.htm

3. http://archive.indianexpress.com/news/sachin-tendulkars-farewell-speech-full-text-no-more-matches-in-my-life/1195836/

4. http://www.nobelprize.org/nobel_prizes/peace/laureates/1979/teresa-lecture.html

5. http://www.youthconnectmag.com/2013/09/21/greatest-speeches-dr-apj-abdul-kalams-speech-hyderabad/

6. http://en.wikipedia.org/wiki/Tryst_with_Destiny

7. http://ibnlive.in.com/news/full-text-swami-vivekanandas-1893-chicago-speech/220148-53.html

8. http://indiatoday.intoday.in/story/narendra-modis-speech-at-ficci-in-ahmedabad/1/343497.html

9. https://www.pminewyork.org/adminpart/uploadpdf/7728001.pdf

10. https://www.facebook.com/notes/gosports-foundation/abhinav-bindras-speech-at-the-gosports-foundation-athletes-con-

clave-2013/559044144137299

11. http://aaspeechesdb.oscars.org/link/081-15/

12. https://thejeshgn.com/wiki/great-speeches/give-me-blood-and-i-promise-you-freedom-subash-chandra-bose/

13. http://specials.rediff.com/news/2007/aug/06slide1.htm

14. http://www.gandhi-manibhavan.org/gandhicomesalive/speech2.htm

15. http://parliamentofindia.nic.in/ls/debates/vol5p1.htm

16. http://www.indiragandhi.org.in/indira-gandhi-speeches.htm

17. http://www.northsouth.org/items_interest/speech_murthy.asp

18. http://specials.rediff.com/getahead/2007/jun/14anand.htm

19. https://www.youtube.com/watch?v=_3HFNqforiM

20. http://www.aima.in/media-centre/publications/Shahrukh-Khan-speech-at-AIMA-NMC.html

21. http://www.azimpremjiuniversity.edu.in/mr-azim-premji%E2%80%99s-speech-et-awards-december-7-2013

22. http://www.deendayalupadhyay.org/

23. http://www.savarkar.org/content/pdfs/en/hindu-rashtra-darshan-en-v002.pdf

24. https://www.marxists.org/archive/bhagat-singh/1930/x01/x01.htm

25. http://indiatoday.intoday.in/story/narendra-modi-independence-day-speech-full-text-red-fort/1/377299.html